AF504693

sale$fuze

How to confidently generate a steadily increasing flow of patient appointments
Brought to you by:
THE DRIVING FORCE

Featuring the industry's only
"You Make Money First"
GUARANTEE

CBS
NBC
abc
HIPAA
FOX
Inc.
WALL STREET JOURNAL

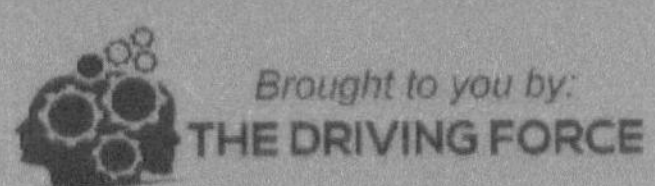

SALESFUZE

How to confidently generate a steadily increasing flow of patient appointments to create a successful thriving practice.

Walter Bergeron
&
Sam Frentzas

SALESFUZE

Trademark ™ 2020 by Driving Force Company LLC

ISBN: 9798677689888

Published by Driving Force Company

Visit the Author Website:

www.DrivingForceCompany.com

Disclaimer

Acknowledgements

<u>Walter Bergeron</u>

I really want to thank one of the people that has been there with me through thick and thin. She encouraged me when I needed to raise my spirits and kicked me in the butt when I needed to get to work and just get it done. The simple words of "thank you" don't express anywhere near enough gratitude for what she has endured to be with me for these two plus decades, but I want her to know that I do truly thank her for being one of the biggest reasons for my accomplishments. Thank you Jana.

Thank you Evan, for allowing me to be a father to an amazing son.

<u>Sam Frentzas</u>

Thank you to my brothers and sisters and my parents for being a family rich in relationships and love.

I am sure I have missed many people and they all deserve

my deepest Thank you. I want to thank the people on this

journey with me. When self-doubt crept in, that wasn't an

option from the highs to the low's she's been my true north

and My Driving Force. Thank you, Peggy.

Thank you, James, for being the son I dreamed of.

Leia, for being the biggest dreamer.

Thank you to my Sister and Brother and Mother

who kicked me in the ass and patted me on the back along

the way.

To my late father James Frentzas, my best friend the

man who took down the path of being who I am today.

You left me with two quotes that will never leave me, when

I wanted to move to California at 18 you said no, you

wanted to raise me you wanted "my handprint on your

heart" I would not be the person I am today if I moved.

You talked about legacy, if I become half the man you are

then I leave this earth the richest man.

I can't name everyone I want to thank and they know who they are, Thank you.

About The Authors

Walter Bergeron

Walter Bergeron is a down to earth, blue-collar, multi-millionaire serial entrepreneur owning and operating as many as six companies simultaneously. Mr. Bergeron is a best-selling author and Marketer of the Year. This US Navy veteran started his entrepreneurial journey at the young age of 12, detailing automobiles in his parents' driveway. In 1996, after he completed a U.S. Navy tour aboard the nuclear-powered aircraft carrier USS Carl Vinson, he started his industrial repair company in a small shed in the middle of the sugarcane fields of Louisiana. His entrepreneurial path has led him to the latest sale of one of his companies for $10 Million. He is now guiding other driven blue-collar entrepreneurs on a path to exponentially grow their business to achieve their own eight figure lifestyle. For a free one on one personal business strategy session with Mr. Bergeron go

to www.DrivingForceCompany.com

About The Authors

Sam Frentzas

 Sam Frentzas grew up in an Entrepreneurial family rooted in his father's belief that you must treat a customer well, and offer a quality product. Spending time with his family is his biggest driver to his continued success. This goes back to even when he was working at his father's clothing stores during the summers and while attending Loyola University. There Sam built a strong work ethic that carried over as a Commodity Trader at the Chicago Mercantile Exchange. During the span of a ten year trading career, Sam also graduated from the Conservatory Program at Second City, performing and writing many sketch comedy acts on stage. In 2005 Sam also became a member of the Screen Actors Guild, which he still belongs to today. Sam's real passion lies in being an entrepreneur. Then he earned the coveted position of Director of Sales for a financial information

company, Sam saw the value in smart marketing and opened his own successful financial information company and takes real pride in helping other entrepreneurs reach their maximum potential. For a free one on one personal business strategy session with Mr. Frentzas go to www.DrivingForceCompany.com

Contents

Introduction

Introduction

How to confidently generate a steadily increasing flow of patient appointments to create a successful thriving practice.

The Agenda

My agenda in our small amount of time we have together while you read this book is to give you little-effort strategies that provide big impact in your practice and life. My aim is to make you lots and lots of appointments for your practice giving you predictable practice revenue, turning you into a patient-focused 'Super Doctor' running a successful, thriving practice.

To give you the best possible chance of having a growing and thriving practice, you need to have a proven system for generating a steady flow of patient appointments for your practice. To do this properly, you'll need a strategy that is able to cover all of the appointment setting and revenue needs of your practice. More appointment means more revenue. What I am about to show you will be a strategy to do just that for your practice so that, probably for the first time, you will be in control and able to create your own economy and thrive.

What I Need From You

Now this is a two-way street. I'm going to give you my A-level best for our brief time we have together while you're reading this because I have faith that you will actually use what I share with you. Nothing pains me more, nothing hurts me deeper, than someone who encounters a life-changing idea and lets it go to waste. So, I'm going to give you my best, but in return I ask you for your best and that means that this book becomes interactive. It doesn't matter what time of the day or night it is that you are reading this, you need to take some action right away.

But first let's make a deal with each other. If I make you a bunch more money first, can I get you to promise you'll spend just a little of that money with me and my company in the future?

Let me know if that's okay with you by texting the letter "Y" to 312-313-1174. Because I'm not letting you get off the hook. I just want to be clear. If I show you how to make a whole bunch of money, and then you, in fact, do make a whole bunch of money, will you spend a little bit of that money with me and my company? If I make you a whole bunch of money, will you just bring some of that back to me? Would that be okay? Go ahead and text the letter "Y" to 312-313-1174 if that is, in fact, okay for you. Remember this book is interactive and if you simply read this and don't take the simplest of actions like texting the letter "Y", then there is no way you'll take the massive action you need to take to make your practice as successful as it can be. Little actions lead to bigger actions, so take

Introduction

this small action right now no matter what time of the day or night it is right now. Don't read another word in this book until you do this.

You didn't achieve your doctorate by simply sitting around, passively reading and listening, you had to do clinical training as well, you had to take action and get some hands on activity in order to reach your level of expertise so that's what I am going to get you to do today.

I don't mean yes in your head, I don't mean yes with a nod I, mean YES with action!

I need you to take some action right now, I need you to grab your cell phone and text 1 little letter Y right now to 312-313-1174.

Text the letter "Y" to 312-313-1174. Just so you know I take this very seriously and we will not move forward until you actually pick up your phone and text the letter Y to 312-313-1174. I'll wait!

While I'm waiting for you, Jim Rohn says this: "There's two pains in life, the pain of discipline or the pain of regret." "You're going to experience one of those two pains with your practice. Do you want to experience the pain of discipline and the success that comes with that or the pain of regret? I'll leave it to you to decide. Text the letter "Y" to 312-313-1174

What I'm about to show you today is so incredibly powerful. I want you to give the attention to it that it deserves because so often – it's hard to know out there, with all the noise and confusion these days, who's real and who's not, what is effective and what isn't effective.

So, what I'm about to show you today is transformative if you take it and run with it. How do I know that? Because I've seen it firsthand.

Transformations

Dr. Regan owns 5 practices in the northeast U.S. and as of the latest version of this book we've scheduled

521 appointments for him resulting in $1,397,500 in patient value for his family.

Now before I get too far into this I am not saying that you are going to get results like these, but I do want to show you what's possible when you take what I am about to show you and run with it. Frankly, this is why we do this and this is what is possible for you and your practice, a 7 figure revenue.

So, would it be ok with you if I showed you how to build an empire of practices for real world wealth creation. Would it?

Marcus Lemonis

You may or may not recognize this business superstar's name. Mr. Marcus Lemonis is the famed star of CNBC's ® "The Profit®" and "The Partner®" as well as CEO of Camping World®, Good Sam® and many other companies.

Marcus is partially the reason why we have been able to be so successful in being able to set appointments so effectively. He has created a billion dollar business empire by using a simple but powerful strategy.

The 3 P's

He calls this strategy the 3 P's.

1. People

2. Process

3. Product

If you have these in place you will reach the profit you are working toward. As a practice owner you've got one of the P's already in place, a great product that genuinely helps your patients live better lives.

Now let me show you how we worked with Marcus, actually paid him $100,000 to show us and our members how to combine their product with a proven process run by the right team of people and help you create an unbeatable combination that all but guarantees you a level of success.

Member Dr. Jimmy

Dr Jimmy owns a single practice and came to us telling us *"I'd just rather not rock the boat and move all of my marketing over to us under one roof. I'd just rather leave things as they are now, after all things aren't that bad. Better to leave things as they are than make a change."* Our reply to him was this: *"So as I see it you want to keep doing the same old things but you want and actually expect a different result. I think some people credit Einstein with that exact phrase where he describes insanity, doing the same things over and over and expecting a different result. So instead of doing the same things, Jimmy let's do something different so you can get a different result."* And that's exactly what he did to reach these results.

What you did in the past, is in the past, let's leave it in the past. Instead let's focus on the future where you can make changes and get better results. Think about it this way. What were you doing before you went to school to become a Chiropractor? Was life that bad? Were things that terrible, no you were surviving. But you wanted MORE, you wanted things to be different, so you took a different action and made a significant improvement to your life through change, and that's exactly what this is, making a significant change for the better just like you've already done, that's why you're a Doctor today isn't it?

Member Dr. Dan

Dr. Dan came to us with a disjointed approach to his marketing. He had text messages going out with one company, and Facebook ads with another company, he had his receptionist making phone calls when she had time, and a website that was a couple years old that he had his brother in law do it as a favor to him. But none of it worked together, none of it operated smoothly and it took so much effort on his part to keep it all going, he was constantly juggling one company then another trying to keep all the balls in the air. For months on end he had no idea if any of it was working because there we huge blocks on his calendar that were just empty and his income suffered because of it. Then he put his trust in us and he closed $270,000.00 in treatments in his practice in just 30 days.

Member Dr. Gary

Dr Gary owns a very small practice and yet he found that size doesn't matter. We scheduled him 223 appointments in the first 90 days of working together. Wouldn't you love to get 223 appts too?

Gary wanted to do seminars and webinars to start marketing to a much larger audience at a time, so he hired another company just to do webinars, but he couldn't make it work in conjunction with his website and the appointment booking software in his office wouldn't handle seminars so everything he was doing was all over the place. Everything he was doing was living in isolation and each piece didn't support each other at first, then once he got everything under one roof then a synergy started to take effect and that's when the success truly started to materialize.

Member Dr. Ashlin

Dr. Ashlin didn't jump into working with us right away either. He was very skeptical. He had used almost a dozen other services in bold attempts to get his appointment book filled consistently.

He had tried to solve this problem before and couldn't. He had failed every time previous and he, like you're probably thinking to yourself right now – *"Hey why should this time be any different?"*

Here's why it's different, because what we did was earn our fee by getting him paid first. The result you see above is what he earned BEFORE he paid us a penny to help him. Results in advance, that's the way you know you are working with someone that is the real deal.

Of course, he was afraid. Of course he was unsure of himself… at first. Then he overcame that fear with success after success until his successes far outweighed his fear and today he has 126 more appointments and $227,250.00 more for his practice than he had before Salesfuze..

In step 2 of the training I am going to get into you'll see too the thing that Dr. Ashlin is using as one of his practice growth tools.

Why you should pay attention

We're the $100 million appointment people, that's why. Our team consistently schedules approximately 4,221 appointments per day and that happens only because of the people and process we have put in place to help our members to create these kinds of results.

In this book you'll discover

- The proper way to fill you appt book month after month with no additional work on your staff

- The number 1 strategy to have your website finally perform the appointment setting work it was supposed to when you first put it up

- The fool proof, fully automated, zero ad spend campaign that reactivates your inactive patients that are currently sitting dormant.

- What every practice owner ought to know about the role their staff should actually fill in their overall marketing system… Hint – you're probably not using their full range of capabilities.

- The dirty little secrets about HIPAA & TCPA compliance that you may be missing and could cost you dearly in legal fees and damages if you aren't careful.

- How to get free access to the step by step formula to create a one to many webinar profit centers most practice owners completely miss out on.

- How to build an empire of practices for real world wealth creation.

The Proven 4 Step Strategy

This is the 4 step, proven process that our most successful and profitable members are currently using to confidently generate a steadily increasing flow of patient appointments to create a successful thriving practice.

1. Start With Patient Reactivation

One of the most frequently overlooked sources of leads to get those new appointments for your practice: your list of inactive patients. Your dormant list of patients, that you've already paid to advertise to and bring through your doors, is a powerful source of new appointments, which in turn means it's a highly profitable source of new revenue that's normally all but forgotten and yet can be a powerful tool to your bottom line if handled correctly.

2. Continue Building By Acquiring New Patients

Next, you'll need to start the process to acquire more new patients, through social media advertising with forever follow-up by real time professional sales agents, to schedule the maximum number of appointments that can be scheduled from a source of brand-new patients.

3. Set Yourself Apart With Celebrity Positioning

The most successful practice owners set themselves apart from their competitors using powerful celebrity positioning. You then need top positioning over your competitors with a published book and then elevating you to celebrity status with a national book launch.

4. Create Real World Wealth

And lastly create real world wealth through empire building strategies.

Now, it's time for you to discover...

Salesfuze™

Chapter 1

Patient Reactivation

Have you ever heard the saying:

"The Money Is In The List?"

As a practice owner you know that more appointments mean more revenue for your practice and one of the most frequently overlooked sources of leads to get those new appointments for your practice is your list of inactive patients. Reactivating your dormant list of patients that haven't scheduled their next appointment with you is the fastest way to kickstart your practice with more appointments even if it's a small list of only a couple of hundred inactive patients, it's still extremely valuable to you.

That means it's a highly profitable source of new revenue that's normally all but forgotten and yet can be the most powerful boost to your bottom line if handled correctly. Your inactive patient list is a source of new appointments that can generate a steady source of revenue that you've already paid for and is actually easier to sell than new leads that you're getting from other lead sources

no matter what size that list is.

We Create an Irresistible Proven Offer

Remember how Marcus Lemonis gave us the strategy of the 3 P's, well this is where the people come into play. How we do this is with the right people. Our team of copywriters researches and customizes an irresistible offer that has proven to work in your area. No need to have your staff worry about proper copywriting or learning how to do marketing on their own, we have a team of professionals ready to get to work for you.

The offer they'll create for you is like….

A candy bar in the check-out line at the grocery store, you may not need it, but you WANT it, so you BUY it. It's an irresistible impulse buy, something they want, not what they need. This offer brings these patients back to your door so you can wow them with your service.

Our member Dr. Anthony uses a one on one phone consult for weight loss as something his patients want, to get them to schedule an appointment to come and see him.

Example Offer:

"Patient Name, it's Ashley at Superior Chiropractic. Have you given up on your weight loss goal? This week only, be 1 of 6 people to get a FREE one on one phone consult with Dr. Anthony and let him create a personalized plan to meet your goal THIS YEAR! ($185.00 ret. value) To claim your FREE voucher reply GOALMET"

Live Text Message Conversations

Then we send these irresistible proven offers via HIPPA compliant texts, so you can feel confident that your patient data is always secure.

You might be asking yourself, why would you only use texts? Well, simple – results! Hey, let's face it currently texting far outperforms any other communication method. Open rates for texts are as high as 98%, and it doesn't matter what age group. My 77-year-old mother has a smart phone and texts me all the time and you'll find that true with any age group. Last year we sent over 23 million emails out and while texts are killing it, emails are clinging to 8 to 10% open rate, meaning that texts are more than 900% more likely to be viewed.

The first text that goes out is your irresistible offer. If they text back anything other than the correct response, a live professional sales agent will respond to them immediately to get them to make an appointment.

Our team are professional and handle the thousands of texts coming in per day, in addition to the follow ups which increases your opportunities to book more appointments. Our live sales agents are USA based *(located in New Orleans and Chicago)*. They are in house and respond to live text conversations in real time to book appointments for you.

The value of fast and live response to texting cannot be overstated when it comes to generating a steady flow of new patient appointments. The reason we do this is because:

- **There's a 10x decrease in your odds of making a contact with a lead after the first 5 minutes; waiting 15 minutes meant losing nearly 91% of your potential leads.**

- **Responding in 5 minutes vs 10 minutes shows a 400% increase in your odds of qualifying a new lead**

- **The #1 preferred channel for customer service in the US is messaging vs telephone calls**

- With 92% satisfaction, live chat is preferred to more traditional channels, like phone or email.

- Live chat leads to a 48% increase in revenue and a 40% increase in conversion rate as opposed to automated chats and emails.

So when your leads   respond correctly with **YESPLEASE (or whatever key phrase is used in the texts**) then they will get a text with a schedule of your appointment times with your logo.

Once they give us an appointment time, and we add it to your practice calendar.

Felicia Tucker, a practice manager, told us *"We had always struggled getting in touch with inactive patients…we would just keep calling and emailing with no response! Yet when your texts went out, we started getting appointments right away"*

And Felicia, like all of our members using this process, get this kind of success because the right people are focusing 100% of their time on getting you appointments. The speed of the text response and the personal touch of our live agents will maximize your opportunities and ultimately the number of appointments we book for you.

100% HIPPAA Compliant

To increase the success of our members we use a fully HIPAA compliant CRM (customer resource management). To maximize our efforts and to get more appointments for our members we know that the CRM must be a comprehensive suite of features and be used to automate you marketing and sales processes. What does this mean? It means that it should include text, email, voicemail, video, website, images, phone calls, call recordings, scheduling software, calendars, webforms, KPI dashboard, complete 3rd party integrations, patient surveys, webinars, seminars, appointments. This is important to make sure all your marketing pieces are working toward the same common goal, more appointments.

Is Your Front Office Staff Bogged Down

And keep in mind that we do all of this for you, reducing the burden on your staff. We set up your CRM with your sales and marketing automation, reducing the burden on your staff. Our people will handle the thousands of texts coming in per day, we handle all of the text follow ups, all of the reminders and all of the rescheduling which increases the appointments we book for you and generates a steady flow of new patient appointments.

Appointment Notifications, Reminder & Cancellations

We send email or text notification to your staff when an appointment is scheduled, cancelled or rescheduled. If we double book you, well first off... What a great problem to have, right? We handle this in one of two ways, depending on your preference. We can immediately rebook them for an alternate time or many of our clients prefer to keep the double booking and just make the time for them when they arrive. We know you staff wear many hats, and just want to help them, but taking on some of their daily duties.

Scheduler

You can use the schedule built into our software and keep all your appointments in one place, no need for multiple software services to schedule your appointments with it's all built into your new process. Again, this is just another way to help your practice with appointment setting.

Forever Follow Up

Something else that makes our members so successful is what we call Forever Follow Up. This is so important because: **80% of sales are made on the fifth through twelfth contact.**

So, my question to you is, are you following up with every lead or opportunity?

We have discovered that roughly only 10% of practices make 3 attempts to contact a lead. This huge disconnect is why forever follow-up is so important.

Many of our members start out like this. They have only a minimal follow up with any lead. So, their conversion rates are really low and that just by putting in place a proper long term follow up process their conversion rates go up exponentially just like these statistics indicate happen. And it makes perfect sense, doesn't it? Because some people just aren't ready to buy right now but that doesn't mean they will never buy. So, we never give up on your leads, we follow up forever giving you the best chances for a new appointment.

Here are some sales statistics to keep in mind when planning your lead or patient follow-up:

- **48% Of Sales People Never Follow Up With A Prospect**
- **25% Of Sales People Make 2nd Contact And Stop**

- **12% Of Sales People Only Make 3 Contacts And Stop**

- **Only 10% Of Sales People Make More Than 3 Contacts**

- **2% Of Sales Are Made On The 1st Contact**

- **3% Of Sales Are Mad On The 2nd Contact**

- **5% Of Sales Are Made On The 3rd Contact**

- **10% Of Sales Are Made On The 4th Contact**

- **80% Of Sales Are Made On The 5th To 12th Contact**

Our member Dr. David said: *"We ran out of spots the first day and had to add more to the calendar with patients that I hadn't spoken to in over 2 years!"*

So this is how we follow up for our members. Once an appointment is scheduled the patients will get a confirmation and a reminder the day before and one last one an hour before their appointment time. Our live agents are there to every step of the way to respond to any questions they may have and keep them excited about their upcoming appointment. Our agents will reschedule them if necessary and take care of any cancellations. If they do cancel and don't reschedule, we keep personally following up with them with new offers to try to get them make another appointment. We know your services are fabulous and make sure that this is conveyed in each message, all trying to make an appointment.

Referral Request

Another key to the success of our members is patient referrals.

On average a referring patient makes an average of 2.68 invites, so by having an automated system in place that consistently asks for referrals you will likely multiple the size of your list. So now for our members we have built in that referral request and someone can forward that offer to 2.68 of their friends. Once the new person texts in our team is responding live within minutes to book your appointments, this is a zero-cost acquisition for your practice because we know how valuable each person is.

Google Review Request

We also realize that competition exists everywhere, and you need every edge you can get over your competitors so getting frequent 5-star reviews is an important way to distinguish your practice so that potential patients choose you over any other option.

Many clients we find have reviews that are 1,2, even 3 years old and that negatively affects their SEO ranking, so we'll get you more frequent Google reviews to help boost your visibility on Google.

Here is an example of a review request:

Here is an example of a review we sent for Dr. Jeff and he was able to replace his $150 per month review wave service quite easily. "Thank you for your business! Would you be so kind to recommend us to your family and friends? https://review.com/I" And when the click

the link it opens on you online Google Review.

Achieve Incredible Results

The bottom line is that putting the right process and

the right people in place is about getting you results! And

all of your results will be at your fingertips on your

performance monitoring dashboard. Full transparency of

your results.

Inspect what you expect. We'll evaluate your

results constantly. We make sure to get with you every 30

days to create new offers for your list to continually re-

engage and bring you more appointments. With our

Performance Monitoring Dashboard, you will be able to

see the success each lead brings to your business with each

individual booking. There is NO CONTRACT, we hold

ourselves accountable with the results in the Dashboard.

You'll always know how many appointments were set, the

exact pipeline value, you'll know how many people

referred somebody, along with every piece of data in your practice.

*"Within just 3 days of launching Salesfuze to **only 400** inactive patients, they booked 12 new appointments with each patient valued at over $6,000.00. We're super excited that we now have someone totally dedicated to responding to our patients!" ~Dr. Chris*

Powerful Mobile App

You will have your Salesfuze app downloaded on your smartphone so you can track everything. Knowing that we don't call in sick. Assured that we don't steal from you. We are professionally trained sales organization solely focused only on booking appointments for you.

Live Life On Your Terms

Even if you're on vacation you can use the mobile app. So, you can rest assured that the old mentality of "If the cats away, the mice will play" will no longer apply to your practice.

And that's just step 1 of the process that you'll use to confidently generate a steadily increasing flow of patient appointments to create a successful thriving practice. Step 2 is to acquire new patients.

Chapter 2

Acquire New Patients

Acquire New Patients

To further increase your practice revenue, you'll need a process to start getting fresh targeted leads for new appointments, we'll do that for you with Facebook Advertising, but not like the Facebook advertising you may be used to.

What Most Practices Are Missing With Facebook

What is frequently missing in the process of most practices that are using Facebook for new leads is a real process to get the right people to come to see you.

We hear it time after time that practices are using Facebook or have done Facebook in the past with a mixed bag of results.

We hear that the leads aren't qualified, they come in to your practice but they can't afford your services. Or maybe if you run seminars we hear that the seminar was full of people that just want a free meal, not real buyers.

And the reason is not that Facebook sucks or that Facebook just doesn't work, it's because the process that was used is not a process at all, it's simply an ad that they threw up on Facebook and then nothing else. There is no qualification, no follow up, no real process at all, it's just a simple single ad. To do it right there must be a process in place.

Picture This

You're patient Bob, is sitting in his office on a Tuesday morning drinking a cup of coffee before he gets his day started, scrolling through Facebook and he sees an ad for getting rid of his knee pain. He reads the ad, clicks the link to get more info about your solution then reads about what you do quickly. Most Facebook advertisers would immediately tell Bob to come in for an appointment and consider Bob a good lead, and that's the problem. Bob isn't a good lead and would come to your office, waste your time and never buy a thing from you. But what if instead of immediately jamming Bob up and telling him he needs to come see you that a live professional sales agent started a quick text conversation with Bob. Texting is a really low barrier way to start a conversation and the agent asks Bob 1 or 2 qualifying questions just to make sure Bob is a good fit. These would be questions you would come up with in the form of an offer. If you offer Bob a solution for knee pain but you only want him to come see you if he's never had knee surgery, then you structure the conversation around that or if you only want Bob to some in if he has a certain type of insurance or type of income level, then you structure the conversation around that. You make sure Bob is the right patient for your practice BEFORE you allow him to book an appointment. That way you get high quality leads and Facebook becomes your salvation and not your frustration.

How It Can Work For You

This is how the process will work for your practice when you become a member. Our award-winning advertising team will work with you personally to craft the perfect message and the perfect angle to be the most magnetic to your target market. We will then help you portray exactly what to say and how to say it in order to cause people to know, like and trust you. Many of our clients tell us that what they really like about our Facebook advertising is that we get them leads just like everyone else, but again, we do 3 things that far surpass what everyone else is going.

Live Conversations

The first thing that's really different than what everyone else is doing is that we have live conversations with these leads, not simply automated non-responsive texts.

This is an added twist to your marketing process that will drive *INSANE* results from Facebook even if you've never had it work for you before.

Instant Response

The second thing that differentiates our process is that we have our team of real live professional sales respond instantly to your new leads.

"Responding instantly shows a 900% increase in your odds of qualifying a new lead vs waiting longer than 15 minutes that shows a potential loss of 91% of your new leads."

Conversations are useless unless they happen quickly, if your past Facebook process wasn't working, look into how quickly they responded with a live conversation to your prospective patients you may find that they take hours or even days or maybe never actually respond to a lead, this laziness is part of the reason so many have trouble with Facebook, but no longer will you have to suffer from that.

Massive Follow Up

Then the third part of the process that you will find very different is that we have a much longer follow up. Research shows that 80% of people buy between the 5th and 12th contact. So, if you aren't following up at least this many times, you're missing 80% of your sales

We will continue to follow up with new and existing leads to help convert them into booked appointments for your practice over and over again. These 3 additional parts of our Facebook process helps turn complete strangers into booked patient appointments and raving fans quickly.

Text Phrase Lead Capture

Each lead prefers to communicate in their own way and by lowering the barrier to communication you increase your response success. If you are doing any other type of advertising you can put the power of this into those ads as well with our Text Phrase Lead Capture. So if your handing out flyers or mass mailing brochures or doing TV or Radio ads or any type of advertising you simply tell them to text a short word or phrase to your new number and it will initiate a conversation with our live agents and you'll get much better results because that text phrase leads to instant response, live agent conversation and then long term massive follow up. This is going to super charge your other advertising.

Seminars & Webinars

The next part of the process to get you new patients is seminars and webinars. We want you to take full advantage of being able to offer your treatments in a one to many environment, webinars are your answer.

Facebook advertising campaign that we do for you to fill your webinar that you do through a zoom webinar platform

Puts you in a position of authority and allows you to educate your patients in a one to many environment. And when you record your webinar you now have an asset for your practice that can be used over and over again without adding any more work to your plate once the first webinar is done plus if you want to add additional educational topics you have that option too. That video can be placed on your website, landing pages, you can use it for social media posts or YouTube videos you can distribute.

Imagine weekly educational webinars on different topics that drive fresh new patients to your door consistently filling your practice and allowing you to sell your services in a one to many environment, month after month.

Webinar Results

Dr. Gene owns a small practice with many appointments driven to him through webinars. The last webinar we put on for him got him 136 opt ins, now that's 136 new potential patients that he's never seen before, and he converted 8.02% of them into paying patients. And he has continued to put on webinars, and he's converted 280 of those leads and counting, into new profitable patients.

New Custom Website

Your website is the first thing people see when they are making the decision on whether to make an appointment with your practice, it's your business' identity.

Take this into consideration: 99% of patients that visit a chiropractic website spend 5 seconds on the "Homepage" and 5 seconds on the "About Us" page before making their decision.

Is your current website good enough to win that battle?

Now maybe this is you. You like your website and you love your webmaster and he'll make any changes you ask him to.

Does your current website, as brilliant as it is, does it confuse a visitor, a confused visitor will simply move on and not make any decision?

Here's a quick check you can do on your home page, open your home page and take 5 seconds and count how many things you are asking your patients to do, how many calls to action on your home page? Is there a phone number to call to get more information, then maybe a download you want them to click on, then maybe a calendar link to book an appointment? Now click off the page and tell me which choice you made. Is there even the slightest confusion or indecision in your mind, of course there is. May I suggest that one single prominent call to action performs much, much better than 2 or 3 or 4 different ones because you eliminate confusion and increase clarity and help them to make a decision faster and easier with a single call to action.

High Converting Website

You need to inform your patients that the issues they have can be solved by you and you alone. Now the task is to create a website catered to informing the world that they are not alone in their situation, and *you* have the answer for which they've been searching.

Mobile Friendly Website

Just because you have a website, doesn't mean that it is optimized for phones and tablets. While it might require a little extra design work, these reasons for a mobile friendly site make it worth it. Google prioritizes mobile-friendly websites over those that are not in mobile search results. The Google algorithm change that occurred in 2015 tweaked the way Google displays mobile search results. Websites that are optimized for mobile rank better than those that don't.

People everywhere use mobile devices to do everything from simple internet searches to purchasing big ticket items and much more. The reason? It's fast and easy. Patients want to connect and get what they're looking for quickly. If you're not optimized for mobile, you can't offer your patients immediate service.

It helps you build credibility with your patients as well as influencers in your specialty. With a mobile friendly website, anyone who tries to visit your site on a mobile device will have a proper experience, and that will encourage them to see you as a credible resource for information, products and services.

It's Becoming A Standard Best Practice

Many websites are mobile-friendly with more and more coming online every day. Responsive web design has made mobile optimization more straight forward and accessible to everyone, and that means users have begun to expect this level of functionality to come standard when browsing on their mobile devices.

You Can Reach More Patients, Faster

Making your website mobile-friendly automatically opens your patient base up to anyone performing a mobile search. And even better, customers won't have to hunt for your site or type in the exact URL to find it – they can just perform a search to find you quickly and easily.

You'll Make Your Patients Happy

When a patient or a potential patient accesses your site to find information or look for something you sell, you want the experience to be nothing short of great. Because many people use mobile devices to access the web, only a mobile-friendly website can promise to offer that experience. Happy patients will return to your site and tell others about how great it is. Unhappy patients will do the opposite.

Google Wants You To Do It

Webmasters know when Google recommends you do something, you should really try to do it. This is the case with making websites mobile-friendly. Google has explained why mobile is so important in their own words, and the number one reason they cite is everyone has smartphones, and they're constantly using them to search.

Your website will look great and function well on any device, provided you use responsive web design to build or redesign your site. Why take chances when it comes to mobile optimization? With responsive design, your website will respond to the mobile device a person is using to access your site, and it will render to look and function well, no matter what.

It Benefits Your Reputation

Not just online, but offline as well. People will take note of a website they have a great experience with – and they will also take note of a website they have a bad experience with. Reputation is everything, and most businesses can't afford to give people a bad experience – digital or otherwise.

Your business will be seen as modern and relevant. You might offer some of the most useful, valuable and unique products or services on the market, but if your website's mobile experience is poor or non-existent, your company will be a digital dinosaur – encouraging people to seek help elsewhere. On the other hand, mobile-friendly websites are contemporary, cutting-edge and legit – they are how you get your foot in the door with anyone that has a smartphone.

Websites that aren't mobile-friendly are quickly falling by the wayside within our fast-evolving digital landscape. As time goes by, more and more websites will emerge that are mobile-friendly, pushing those that are not even further down the search results page and away from customers.

Your Patients Are Using Mobile Devices

The number 1 most important reason you need a responsive website is that your customers are using their mobile. <u>57% of all web traffic</u> is done on mobile devices. More than half of your customers are checking you out from their smartphones. What kind of experience are you giving them?

Builds Trust

Here's that same percentage again. 57% of online users say they won't recommend a business with a poorly designed mobile website.

Yes. It's that big of a deal to have a mobile-friendly website. It's silly to risk losing customers and referrals based on something you can easily fix.

Be Competitive

If having a responsive website for mobile devices isn't a top priority for you, beware. Your top competitors have probably already made sure that their site is mobile friendly. And which business do you think your customer is going to choose when browsing from their smartphone?

Amplify Your Visibility

One of the best things about having a mobile-friendly website is that you can reach a wider audience. Responsive websites make online sharing simple and so your web visitors are more likely to share on their social platforms.

Plus, mobile-friendliness is a ranking symbol on Google. That means that mobile-friendly websites appear higher in search results.

Having a responsive website is a free way to rank better on search engines. Why wouldn't you want to take that opportunity? The more organic search results, the more leads and conversions – it's as simple as that.

Keep Their Attention

In our instant, digital age, people now have a shorter attention span than goldfish. Sad but true. One aspect of a mobile-friendly website is that it loads quickly. You can't afford to have a website that takes longer to load. Your customers will click off your page in a heartbeat. In fact, more than half of mobile web visitors will leave your site if it takes more than 3 seconds to load. Don't lose a large chunk of potential customers. Make your website responsive.

Better Browsing Experience for Your Visitors

What's the main difference between mobile friendly and responsive websites and those that aren't?

The customer's experience. A mobile-friendly website gives your website visitors a visually appealing, enjoyable encounter with your company.

Site navigation is simple and intuitive. Sharing content is natural and easy. Best of all, the site loads quickly, and the text is easy to read and fits on the small screen.

Make it Easy for Customers to Contact You

The more convenient it is for customers to reach you, the more likely they are to do it. Having a mobile-friendly website means that your email address and phone number are easy to find and clickable. All your customers have to do is click and the phone will start ringing. This is better for your customers and for you because it will likely lead to a sale.

Mobile Users Buy More

Mobile is convenient. There's little load time, no waiting around for devices to start up, and, as the name suggests, it's mobile. Mobile-friendly sites can be accessed from pretty much anywhere which helps with impulse buys. People aren't hanging on to the idea of purchasing when they get home on their PC – they want to do it now! Accessible websites enhance the customer experience. The better the experience, the more likely they are to purchase – and the stats back that up.

On average, 15% of desktop users make purchases at least once a week, whereas 35% of mobile users make purchases at least once a week. If they hit a website that is hard to navigate on mobile or doesn't feel intuitive, they'll take their business elsewhere – and with the power of mobile they'll be making that purchase with your competitor in about 30 seconds.

It's Cost Effective

Responsive website design ensures that webpages adapt to the device it is being viewed on to ensure a consistent structure and experience. This is important because without responsive design sites either look outdated or will load different adaptations which increase the design and maintenance costs.

More so, it massively improves search engine optimization which will make a huge difference to the marketing budget. Almost 60% of Google searches are made on mobile phones, so Google doesn't like websites that are not mobile-optimized and punishes those sites by pushing them down the search results.

Social media advertising also benefits from improved efficiency and efficacy from mobile optimization. Take Facebook, for example. Over 90% of Facebook users access the service with a mobile device.

Social media is a time-filler; when people are commuting, waiting in line, avoiding the advert break, or enjoying an antisocial lunch to get away from Brian who hasn't stopped talking about his latest muscle car restoration project – we get it Brian, you build cars as a hobby – and the mobile phone is an easy and readily available distraction.

So when people are clicking your links on social media, they want to travel seamlessly to a site that doesn't look like 2004 threw up on it.

User Experience

User experience is everything these days. A positive experience is accessing an intuitive site that doesn't require users to pinch and zoom to find something or build up frustration trying to navigate to a page the user knows they can get to in a single click on their PC. Frustration will send visitors to mobile-optimized competitors and the chances of winning them back are slim with Google figures showing that 61% of users are unlikely to return to a site they found difficult to access.

Mobile optimization avoids the unnecessary loss of customers and deals with the scourge of all Internet marketing campaigns: user impatience. Consumers have been spoiled with convenience and speed for so long that, according to Kissmetrics, a single second delay in website loading time can see a 7% reduction in customer conversions.

Google standards dictate that a webpage should load in two seconds. A responsive site can do that; a desktop site loading on a mobile device has no chance.

Search Engine Optimization

Your website needs to be filled with backlinks for SEO purposes. You need to feature the proper keywords for SEO. You need messaging continuity between your Social Media, Website, and Marketing campaigns. Salesfuze is your one stop shop. Do you want to stop spending extra money and nickel and diming your way to the poor house by working with a multitude of companies?

That's the first 2 steps of the process that you'll use to confidently generate a steadily increasing flow of patient appointments to create a successful thriving practice. In step 1 you reactivated your inactive patients list to immediately generate sales for you, in step 2 you start acquiring new patients and now in step 3 you are going to uniquely position yourself above and beyond your competitors.

Chapter 3

Celebrity Positioning

Uniquely position yourself above and beyond your competitors.

To elevate you to a celebrity status and uniquely position yourself above and beyond your competitors you are going to need a newly published book with a national book launch.

I would like you to take a minute and image what your prospective patients would think of you if they see your new book:

On your website

On Amazon

In your waiting room

On Facebook

In a Press release

Handed to them in person at a local event

Published Book

We create and publish a book on Amazon and Kindle for our members so they can be the ACE in their field, the Authority, Celebrity and Expert in their field.

Let's think long-term practice growth like our member Dr. Brent is doing. How many doctors in your area are published authors? Imagine being a published author with a new book launched to a national audience. What would that do for your local authority and credibility?

A published book that has national exposure gains you instant credibility like Dr. Steve. It will give you exposure that will be featured in national media giving you a huge boost in positive impact and reputation.

But why stop at one, what about a whole series like our member Dr. Jim. His two books help him stand out from the competition and show him as an expert in his field.

Plus, it can also add passive income to you and your practice. Now your goal is not to make $20,000 by selling your book directly as a published author. Your goal is to make $1 million by giving your book away. Having people raise their hand and gaining instant credibility by attracting your ideal patient. You can even raise your fees by becoming that expert in your field and getting more publicity.

National Book Launch

A published book that has national exposure gains you instant credibility giving you a huge boost in positive impact and reputation. We will write and distribute a national press release for you. You'll use variations of your press release in all of the other marketing materials you'll create for your book like your blog or any and all of your social media channels. Your media kit will be done, too and can now include major media credentials to boost your authority and credibility you have in your market! A press release gets you seen on CNBC, NBC, ABC, Fox, Newsweek, all these news channels and give your name an instant high level of credibility.

As the news stories featured in newspapers, magazines, news sites and blogs have a positive impact on your reliability, image and reputation, they also help you to be recognized in your industry, business circles and create a positive branding perception within the organization as well.

Search Engine Optimization

On top of the national exposure your book and press release will boost your Search Engine Optimization. This is the art and science of getting book pages to rank higher in search engines such as Google. Because search is one of the main ways in which people discover content online, ranking higher in search engines can lead to an increase in traffic to a website. Your new book combined with your national press release is going to get you better SEO rankings.

Reach Your Target Audience

Communicating with the target audience though print and online mediums can have a longer lasting effect on brand recognition. When readers see your name in a medium that publishes content aimed at your target audience, it would have a better impact in terms of your brand image and reputation.

Chapter 4

Empire Building

Empire Building

Practice growth doesn't start and stop with getting more appointments and improving your marketing and sales. There is a much higher level of strategy that needs to go into building an empire of practices for real wealth creation.

Imagine

Imagine owning, operating and cashing in on 1, 2, 5 or 15 practices running and generating multi-generational wealth for you and your family. That all starts with expanding your horizons and seeing the true possibilities that are out there, waiting for you to take hold of.

Driving Force University

With Driving Force University, you gain access to real world experience and training delivered to you by an 8-figure master level strategist that has already done this, guiding you every step of the way through this university.

Now in the past this has been accessible only to our mastermind members that pay $50,000.00 per year to be a member, which currently is sold out and we aren't yet taking applications for next year, but you can still tap into the knowledge of how to build your new empire of practices so you are able to create true wealth in your life.

Business Models To Achieve Massive Business Growth

These 6 business models will help to erase the need for you to take years and years to grow your practice to the level that you dreamed of the day you opened your doors for practice or put your shingle out and started to accept patients for profit. They will forever end the need for you to follow the typical slow growth model that you see everyone else in your industry using. They will allow you to grow your practice hundreds of times faster than 99.99% of the 28.8 million US businesses that are only growing at an average rate of a miniscule 7.8% per year and follow the path that the fastest .01% of businesses are doing to grow at an average of 1,772%.

The training programs behind these 6 business models have helped hundreds of our clients to identify their biggest growth opportunities and dreams and then connect them with the resources they needed to make those dreams become a reality. This includes clients who have payed $100,000 or more for done for you marketing programs, and over $12,000 for a single day of consulting.

The Criteria

The best way to maximize your massive growth is to use only business models that meet these three criteria.

Criteria One

First, the business model must be highly leverageable. Meaning that it must be a business model that allows you to put in a small effort and get really big output. Preferably a business model that allows you to take an action once and get returns on that investment of your time and energy and effort for a long, long time.

Criteria Two

Secondly, the business model should also be highly scalable. Meaning that it has the potential to scale up to something huge. It must be capable of far surpassing any of your current growth goals and supply you with growth for a long time from now. There is no sense in pursuing business growth that doesn't have the ability to scale up to something large enough for you to get excited about it and be worth the time and effort you are going to put into making this a reality.

Criteria Three

Lastly, the business model must be complementary to what you are already doing. It's got to add value and bolt-on to your core business so that it becomes a cash-pumping oil well much more easily than if you had to start a new venture from scratch and learn the hard way all the lessons of a new industry or skill. Better that you already know the industry, be familiar with the skills you need so that you already have a head start.

Business Model #1 – Expert Course

This is the place you need to start. You need to turn your core expertise into a training course. This business model is sometimes referred to as an information product in some circles. The training course, your Expert Course, can be divided into multiple modules and delivered online and/or offline in the form of videos, audios, written transcripts, worksheets, process maps, etc. Any media that delivers the training in the best way for the student to absorb the information and achieve the result promised from the training.

How does this business model help to achieve massive business growth? You may be asking yourself …

Well, it meets all of the criteria we just talked about. It is highly leverageable, highly scalable, complements just about any type of business in any type of industry.

For example:

Our inner circle member, Gene, owns a gunsmith training company and like most business owners Gene started with a simple idea. Gene wanted to simply train gunsmith hobbyists better ways to enjoy their hobby in his region of the country.

Then Gene applied the Massive Business Growth formula (MV+XR=MRG) to expand his idea into a Massive Vision (MV), to train 100,000 U.S. veterans 10 different blue-collar skills to enable them to become more employable and have additional highly valuable skillsets. Gene then continued using the Massive Business Growth formula (MV+XR=MRG) and connected to an eXtraordinary Resource (XR) of the U.S. Army training command to get his valuable training into the right hands on a national scale instead of his original idea of simply regional training.

So for Gene, by first using the Massive Business Growth formula (MV+XR=MRG) and then bolting an Expert Course business model to his existing business, he transformed a business that was only able to generate revenue in his local area into a business that is now highly leverageable because he only needs to record and generate the training program one time and he can sell it over and over and over again. A business that is highly scalable because he can now sell his training internationally, and it complements what he was already doing. The end result is that he is on his way to reaching his own Massive Business Growth by applying the formula (MV+XR=MRG) to the first of 6 ideally suited business models.

Business Model #2 – Recurring Revenue

After you have your Expert Course up and running an making a profit then you bolt on business model #2, the

Recurring Revenue business model. This business model turns your core expertise or your business' services into a monthly membership program so that you start off each month with money coming in instead of starting back at zero like everyone else does. You break down your knowledge or your service into bite sized chinks that you feed to your customers every month. This business model is highly leverageable, highly scalable, complements just about any type of business in any type of industry.

For example:

Gamefly breaks its service down into multiple levels of monthly memberships which provide it with recurring revenue, so does LegalShield as well as Concirege Choice Physicians.

Another example from a Salesfuze member:

Tim started with a simple idea to help his local customers do a better job trimming their trees. Then he applied the Massive Business Growth formula

(MV+XR=MRG) to expand his idea into a Massive Vision (MV) to nationally train all private homeowners how to transform their yards into stunning showplaces using only a compass and the sun. Using the Massive Business Growth formula (MV+XR=MRG), his vision went from local to national.

Tim then continued using the Massive Business Growth formula (MV+XR=MRG) and connected to an eXtraordinary Resource (XR) of his statewide Chamber of Commerce that endorsed his program. His massive revenue growth was achieved by connecting a membership program to a much larger vision of what his business can be.

So, for Tim, by first using the Massive Business Growth formula (MV+XR=MRG) and then bolting a Recurring Revenue business model to his existing business, he transformed a business that was only able to generate revenue in his local area into a business that is now highly leverageable because he only needs to record and generate the training program one time and he can sell it over and over and over again. A business that is highly scalable because he can now sell his training nationally and it also feeds his tree trimming service business, and it complements what he was already doing. The end result is that he is on his way to reaching his own Massive Revenue Growth by bolting on their business model to what he was already doing.

Business Model #3 – Consulting

A Consulting business model is another strategy to turn your knowledge, advice, or service into revenue. The most profitable method to do this is somewhat like the recurring revenue model, meaning that to keep the revenue reliable the client needs to receive the consultations on a regular basis.

Inc. 500 Examples

DayBlink Consulting uses the Massive Business Growth formula (MV+XR=MRG) and applies it to a consulting business model to provide strategic and executive advisory services designed to teach leaders to deliver advisory services, think and act entrepreneurially, and give back to the community in a meaningful manner. They are #159 on the fastest growing U.S. companies list for 2017 with a growth rate of 2,551% and a revenue of $6.9M

Thought Logic Consulting uses the Massive Business Growth formula (MV+XR=MRG) and applies it to consulting business model to provide consulting in a range of areas, including mergers and acquisitions, organizational change, analytics, and strategy. They are #57 on the Inc. 5000 fastest growing U.S. companies with a growth rate of 5,745% and 7.8M in revenue.

GrowthPlay uses the Massive Business Growth formula (MV+XR=MRG) and applies it to a consulting business model to provide business consulting in the areas of staffing, messaging, and coaching. They are #22 on the Inc. 5000 fastest growing U.S. companies with a growth rate of 9,935% and 29.3M in revenue.

Blueprint Consulting Service uses the Massive Business Growth formula (MV+XR=MRG) and applies it to a consulting business model to provide business management and IT services consulting. They are #161 on the Inc. 5000 fastest growing U.S. companies, with a growth rate of 2,538% and 47.1M in revenue.

Business Model #4 – Mastermind

A Mastermind business model is a coordination of knowledge and effort of two or more people who work toward a definite purpose in a spirit of harmony. It's also a way for its' members to gain unfettered access to input from some of the best and the brightest in their industry.

You can find them in any industry, if you want to do a quick search on Google, you can find mastermind groups everywhere you look. Now, they don't necessarily call themselves masterminds in every case. For one example, in the basket weaving community, masterminds are a place that they get together called guilds. For example:

A mentor of mine, Mr. Dan Kennedy runs multiple mastermind groups, of which I have been a part of for many years. His mastermind group is called the Titanium Info Marketing Mastermind. They meet 3 times a year, Dan does one on one hot seat style consulting and gives them advice on their info business problems and goals and then lets the group of other members give input to the individual on the hot seat.

What can be so great about this more advanced business model is that you can combine business models to make this more profitable. In the case of Mr. Dan

Kennedy, he uses his mastermind members, who pay him upwards of $33,000.00 to be a member, to also participate in his other services. His mastermind members can use his one on one consulting services for $19,000 per day or they can hire him to do high level copywriting services for $100,000 plus. So by using these higher level business models as bolt-on revenue centers for your business, give some thought into how you can use them to support other parts of your business and especially think about how they can support the other business models we are talking about here in this book.

Another example:

Sam and I run a mastermind called The Driving Force Mastermind for $25,000 per member. We meet 3 times a year and focus specifically on the Massive Business Growth Formula (MV+XR=MRG) and work one on one with members to make sure they achieve the growth they want from their businesses. We also have members that have ascended from our Expert Course as well as our recurring revenue programs. So, we intermingle all of the business models into one super-fast growing business by applying the Massive Business Growth Formula to business models that are all highly leverageable, highly scalable and complement what we are already doing.

Business Model #5 – Software Creation

A Software Creation business model is an advanced business model in which you solve the problems of your customers with software. Now, before you dismiss the use of software because you don't want to learn to program code or you think hiring programmers and developers is way too costly, let us put your mind at ease. The creation of software is simply another great tool to use to solve the problems of your customers in a unique way that sets you apart from any of your competitors. Plus, if you start small then gradually improve your software the cost is relatively small since the price and availability of programming experts has gone down substantially over the last few years. This is a business model that is for the more advanced business expert but worth the effort because of its leveragability, scalability and how easily it can complement what you already do to solve your customers' problems.

Inc. 500 Examples

Skillz uses the Massive Business Growth formula (MV+XR=MRG) and applies it to a software business model, they developed a mobile platform that enables users to host streaming video game tournaments and to interact directly with other fans of live sporting events. They are #1 on the fastest growing U.S. companies list for 2017 with a growth rate of 50,059% and a revenue of $54.2M

Automotive Mastermind uses the Massive Business Growth formula (MV+XR=MRG) and applies it to software and mastermind business models. They developed a predictive analytics and marketing automation technology for the automotive industry. They are #7 on the Inc. 5000 fastest growing U.S. companies with a growth rate of 17,675% and $23.2M in revenue.

An Example From One Of Our Inner Circle Members

Mike owns a company where he provides direct mail services to his clients in the HVAC contracting industry and Mike started with a simple idea. He wanted to simply mail postcards for his HVAC contractor clients in his region of the country.

Then Mike applied the Massive Business Growth formula (MV+XR=MRG) to expand his idea into a Massive Vision (MV) to use his software, that uses advanced mathematical and census data to predict when customers in an area are most likely to need HVAC services, and give this software away to sell his high end mailing services to every HVAC contractor in the U.S.

So, for Mike, by using the Massive Business Growth formula (MV+XR=MRG) and applying it to a software business model using his existing business, he transformed a business that was very much like every other marketing mailing company into a business that is now highly leverageable because he has a unique software model that no other business owner in his industry has access to that he created once and can use to sell his customer s over and over again. He created a business that is highly scalable because he can now sell his services much more easily nationally, and it complements what he was already doing because he already needed to do lots of back end data mining, but now it's neatly packaged into a software for use of his customers exclusively. The end result is that he is on his way to reaching his own Massive

Revenue Growth at the 9-figure level by applying the formula to an ideally suited business model.

Business Model #6 – Business Stacking

A Business Stacking business model is the process of strategically buying other complementary, not identical, businesses to grow your business very large, very quickly. It is a three-step process. Step one is to strategically acquire another complementary business. Step two is to apply the cross-marketing multiplier and step three is to use efficiency profits. With these three steps, it is possible to grow a business by over 500% in as little as 12 months.

An Example From One Of Our Clients

Gerald owns a pest control company that was grossing around $600k in annual revenue and around 10% profit. Gerald's first step was to seek out and strategically buy other companies and merge them with his company. Then he would use 3 growth models and exponentially grow his company and then sell the much larger, much more profitable company after he reached his growth goal.

For Gerald, that process looked like this:

He found for a company that:

1. Had around the same gross revenue as his company, so he could afford to do this deal comfortably.

Actually, the way this deal was structured Gerald walked away from the closing with many thousands of dollars in his pocket, through a process called a full leveraged buyout.

2. Had the same type of clients but no overlap between his current clients and the acquisition company clients

3. He made sure there was lots of duplication of company business processes.

And I'll get into why he wanted that in a second.

Once he found a company that met these three goals he made the purchase.

Gerald made a… Strategic Acquisition

At closing his <u>$600k business became a $1.2 million company</u>, not a bad day to be able to double the size of your company at the stroke of a pen.

But this is just the tip of the iceberg when it comes to massive growth through Growth-Stacking.

Step two of Growth-Stacking is called the… Cross Marketing Multiplier

Do you remember when I told you that Gerald bought a company that met his goals? You might have noticed that none of his goals for his Strategic Acquisition of the right company had anything to do with the type of services they offered, just that they had identical client types.

Gerald actually bought an air conditioning company. Now Gerald certainly could have bought another pest control company, to most entrepreneurs this would be the most logical choice, stick with what you know.

But Gerald was thinking strategically and used Growth Stacking to maximize the amount of his growth.

He knew that by acquiring another company and focusing on the clients, that the services weren't critical criteria for the purchase. As a matter of a fact, had Gerald bought another pest control company <u>he would not have been able to take advantage of the Cross Marketing Multiplier.</u>

The Cross Marketing Multiplier Works Like This

Gerald took his pest control services and offered those services to his newly acquired clients and in a very short time, since he already had a great relationship with his clients from the purchase of the new business, he quickly increased his revenue by another multiple. Gerald marketed his pest control service to the air conditioning clients and went from $1.2 million to $1.8 million.

But Gerald certainly didn't stop there.

He then took his newly acquired air conditioning services and offered those services to his pest control clients. And since he had a great relationship with those clients as well Gerald's company went from $1.8 million to $2.4 million. This is something absolutely possible when using massive growth through Strategic Acquisition. There is no faster or easier way to double the size of your client list AND have that very critical already established bond, that well developed relationship with your clients, all with the stroke of a pen. And it is because of this previously established relationship that the Cross Marketing Multiplier works. But Gerald didn't stop there either. Remember that one of Gerald 's criteria for the company he was going to buy was that they had a duplication of business processes, meaning that both companies had a human resources department and accounting and sales and marketing departments and personnel and equipment. Well, as a savvy entrepreneur,

Gerald implemented step three of growth-stacking called…Efficiency Profits

Efficiency profits increases growth by another multiple by eliminating all of the duplication between the two companies. By eliminating duplicate expenses in personnel, real estate, business equipment, this change increases profits substantially. Then on top of the elimination of expenses you add back in efficiency by keeping the best of the best parts of both business processes. These two factors enabled Gerald to add another multiple of value to the company while at the same time increasing profits by another 10%.

Summary

Part one, Gerald did one Strategic Acquisition and on day one at the closing he doubled the size of his company from $600k to $1.2 million and walked out of the deal with no up-front costs and with a few thousand dollars in his pocket by doing a fully leveraged buyout.

Part two, Gerald implemented the Cross Marketing Multiplier and within a few months he had cross-marketed the services of both companies, since he now had a list of clients that doubled in size at the closing.

So, he went from $1.2 million to $1.8 million by selling air conditioning services to pest control clients and then went from $1.8 million to $2.4 million by offering his pest control services to his air conditioning clients.

Then part three, he implemented Efficiency Profits and eliminated duplicate expenses and increased the efficiency of both companies and went from $2.4 million to $3 million dollars. So, with Growth Stacking his business size increased by 5 times and his profits went from 10% of $600k, so $60k to 20% of $3 million, that's $600k.

That's 1000% business growth

That's the power of a properly executed, well-engineered massive growth strategy.

And now since Gerald was more experienced in the Growth Stacking process he did this once more and this time shot the size of his business up to over $12 million.

No Promises Here

Now I want to emphasize that I cannot promise or guarantee that you can do this, you need to make this decision and decide if this is right for you. But I would urge you to do a little homework and look at how fast-growing companies are making huge moves. Look at what venture capitalists are doing and look at what the large players in your market are doing to achieve massive growth and market share. I think you will find that strategic acquisitions play a large role and that it would be a great opportunity for you to exponentially grow your business.

You Now Know

You now know that if you want to grow your business fast, then you can't keep doing what everyone else is doing and expect fast growth. You now know it takes the same amount of work to grow slowly with a small idea as it does to grow quickly with a Massive Vision (MV). You now know that you simply can't settle for an ordinary resource. You must seek and use eXtraordinary Resources (XR) to get you there. You know now continuing to try to do this alone is what's holding you down with mediocre growth and mediocre results. You must begin now to apply the Massive Business Growth formula (MV+XR=MRG) if you ever hope to achieve the massive revenue growth that will allow you to live this massively fulfilling lifestyle you deserve.

Chapter 5

Why Not?

So now let me ask you a few questions.

Do you feel more confident that you can get more appointments by harnessing the powers of a complete marketing system in your practice?

Were you happy you came you read this book today?

Do you realize the advantage you now have in the market by just using these 4 steps?

Can you see yourself using what I showed you today to help you set more appointments and grow your practice?

Even if you used just a tiny fraction of what I showed you, would you say your time reading today was well spent?

Would you like to go even further than our limited time it took you to read this book to get into this?

Two Choices

Now, here's what I know about you. Even if we had more time together instead of just the time it took you to read to this point, it's going to be hard, almost impossible, to create lasting change, to give you the full extent and benefit of all that I could give you. No matter how good anyone is – and I'm better than most – one measly book isn't going to go about creating the change in your life that you want and deserve. You need more than that. While what I've given you today was incredibly valuable, as you have just told me, it's frankly the tip of the iceberg. And if you like what I've shared with you thus far, you'll love what I've got for you next if you say to yourself that you want to go even further than our brief encounter today.

You see, before writing this book, I was faced with one of two choices. The first choice is I can share what I've shared so far, part ways with you and then hope that you, on your own, can make a go at it and hopefully succeed, or here's my second option. I can take a more active role and almost 100% responsibility for your success, to create a situation where our relationship could evolve from a more one-and-done type of deal to an ongoing, growing, and mutually rewarding relationship. I chose the second option. When you see what I have in store for you, you'll be glad that I did.

Guarantee You Make Money First, Then You Pay Us!

We're going to work for you for free until we get you 10 appointments that you otherwise wouldn't have gotten on your own.

I'm not asking you to decide yes or no today. I'm asking you to make a fully informed decision, that's all. And the only way you can make a fully informed decision is from the inside and let us prove it to you that this actually works like we say it does. So, you can get on the inside for free. We will get you 10 brand new high value appointments at no cost to you whatsoever so you can see if everything we say in this book is true and valuable enough to you. Then, if it is, that's when you can decide to keep it. If it's not for you, no hard feelings.

How that works is that you get Salesfuze for free today and we get to work immediately to get you 10 appointments. That's right we're going to work for you for free until we get you 10 appointments that you otherwise wouldn't have gotten on your own. You will then, after getting all of these appointments, be able to make a fully informed decision that this is or isn't for you. But you can't make that decision right now for the same reason that you don't buy a house without first taking a look at the inside. That's our YOU GET PAID FIRST Guarantee. Then you decide if this service is worth it per month, then and only then will you happily pay us. Worst case is you get 10 appointments for you practice that you otherwise would never get and we do all the work to get them for you. You keep the appointments, you keep the patient, you keep the money you get from these appointments, you literally have nothing to lose and you have 10 appointments to gain.

Now I know you might be saying to yourself that you really like Salesfuze and all it can do for you and your practice, but you just can't afford it right now. It's simply not in the budget at this time. Then I need to ask you this question. If you could afford it, would you get it? If money wasn't an option, then would you get it?

How much is the average sale worth to your practice? $2000

What is your conversion percentage? 20%

How much money would your practice earn from an additional 10 appointments per month? $4000, so then the MINIMUM value of Salesfuze to you is $4000 per month.

Listen. If Salesfuze required an inhuman amount of time to make successful, I might have three people that

I could point to and say they were members and benefitted from it. But you see, we have hundreds of doctors and staff that have shared with us their successes, and wouldn't you agree with me, it's more people than you've ever seen reading this book before, who have been successful with our marketing solution for doctors? Do you think all these people just had an abundance of time laying around to stop the entire staff doing what they were doing to take these pictures? No, they were so excited about the results that they decided it was worth the time to let us know and others know how well this worked for them and how well it could work for you?

Listen. Salesfuze membership won't cost you any money, it'll actually save you a bunch of money. Here's this. I want you to pull out a piece of paper. Grab a pen. I want you to think of the five things your practice does on a regular basis to get you more appointments. Write any 5 marketing services that you pay for right now, and I want you to write them down. I want you to write the thing that you spend the most money on for marketing your practice as number one; the second most money, number two; the third and three; the fourth and fourth; and the fifth one and the fifth.

So, let's look at #5 the thing that you spend money on that you put your least amount of money into – you might only pay $100, maybe even less. I don't care – what's number five? Is it texting services, is it your website maintenance, is it Facebook advertising, is it Google reviews, is it pay a staff member to make follow up calls, is it some sales training program, is it an appointment calendar software, is it an email sending service, is it to build a new website… Whatever number five is, here's what you do next. Take a big red marker and cross that out. In its place, write 'Salesfuze.' Congratulations. Now, without any more money, I've delivered a solution to you to actually reduce your costs to use Salesfuze and you still get it all. And here's the good thing that you're going to find out. This will actually save you money. Instead of doing whatever you're doing on number five on your own, you're going to be doing it with Salesfuze. So, you'll be able to do it with half the money you're paying now. I've literally given you the money that's going to increase your revenue and build you a thriving practice. That's the best part.

You've already invested time with me today. Don't tell me you don't have the time. If you can make the time to read this far, I guarantee you can make the time to make this successful for you. So, don't give me that. It's not a time issue. It's probably a fear issue. The fear that this won't work for your practice and the fear of the investment. But the doctors we work with had the same fears, and throughout this book you have seen what success they have experienced, this could be you if you choose to move forward with us.

But I have to be honest with you, this may not work for you, but that is why we are offering you the "You make money first, then you pay us" guarantee, to see if this will work for you. And if you do not achieve the success that you are looking for, no problem and no hard feelings, and we will part as friends.

When you're sitting here today, honestly, you've got three options. You could spend no money, do nothing; you could spend your money somewhere else; or you could spend money on this.

Now, here's what I know about doing nothing. Aristotle had the greatest quote. Do nothing, say nothing, be nothing. That's not really an option for a Doctor like you.

Listen. I don't know if there are alternatives that give you a comprehensive suite of done-for-you digital marketing services giving you predictable practice revenue every month out there in the market. There very

 Chapter 5/Why Not?

well might be by other services. But here's what I do know. You're not reading their book right now; you're reading my book. You're spending time with me, and you've been engaged with me all this way for this amount of time. And I don't know about the experience that they can give you and what they can exchange for your money in terms of value, but I do know what we can. We control that, and we take that very seriously. So, the reality here is, if you leave, you don't invest, you put all this time into learning more and you have nothing to show for it and then you try to go somewhere else and find a magical solution, is that likely going to serve you? And the answer is, it's not.

So, you and I have to get serious with each other right now. You've already invested. Doesn't it make sense to continue with a good investment? You had a good experience with us today, didn't you? Yes. You saw value, and you enjoyed learning new ways that a comprehensive suite of done-for-you digital marketing services can give you predictable practice revenue every month; right? Yes. So now it's time to put the money in place to really truly start making the difference. And you can do that by letting us get 10 appointments for you.

We didn't design Salesfuze to see how cheap we could make it for you, we didn't sit back and say what's the bare minimum we could put into this product to sell it at the cheapest price to help the most people the least amount. NO, we designed it to give you the best solution for the greatest deal and that's what you have here, the greatest deal for everything you get with Salesfuze. There is a big engine under this hood as you can tell from everything you're getting.

We take this investment seriously; this is a serious investment because it is a serious solution for your practice.

If it could fill your appointment book month after month and make your practice thrive, then did it really cost you anything? More importantly, what's the cost of inaction?

Maybe you're saying to yourself - I am already doing some of this and quite happy with my results and not sure if the rest of the things you're doing are worth switching over.

Isn't that really the problem. You have company A doing your texting, Company B doing your Facebook ads, Company C is scheduling some appointments for you, Company D has a software gadget that you like to use but it doesn't work with Company A and then Company B doesn't work past 5 o'clock and Company E has a great solution but used to be a part of Company A and they don't work together any more and more drama than a soap opera trying to get 1 single solution that actually does everything you need it to do? So wouldn't you rather just get rid of all the drama and headaches of splitting your time and money between 12 different solutions and instead enroll in 1 solution that does it all, more effectively, more efficiently all under one roof.

Chapter 6

Practice Growth Tunnel Vision

Overcoming Practice Growth Tunnel Vision

Walter Bergeron

In this interview between the Sam Frentzas and Walter Bergeron we want to cover a topic that we call Practice Growth Tunnel Vision. We call it this tunnel vision because it seems like there's people think that there's really only one way to grow their practice and we are going to cover how to overcome and even eliminate that tunnel vision that we as entrepreneurs so easily find ourselves trapped within. It is really because this tunnel vision that we get trapped into this small growth model instead of opening our mind open our vision wider to all the possibilities for massive growth.

We find ourselves in this tunnel vision mode restricting ourselves to only using one or two small ways to grow our business because of two major reasons.

Now the first reason for this small growth tunnel vision is fear based.

We intentionally only view the growth of our business in small ways because of fear, fear of ridicule fear of failure fear that we can't succeed because we've never succeeded that way in the past and we're going to overcome all these things.

So stick with us through this training.

And then the second reason that we as entrepreneurs get this small growth tunnel vision is because of a lack of awareness and ignorance to all the possibilities.

Normally we don't intentionally mean to ignore things and ignore this opportunity to see a wider view of massive growth but we just don't know what we don't know.

And this lack of awareness is keeping you in this minuscule growth mode because of this severely limited vision of what you could accomplish if your mind was wide open to all the growth possibilities that are normally available to you.

All the growth possibilities that are right here at your fingertips right now. And so that's why really 80 percent of massive growth success is psychological, and mindset driven.

And 20 percent is mechanical. 20 percent is tactical. So, if you ask every professional athlete about their own massive successes, they're going to tell you that only a part of it has to do with the mechanics of throwing the football or throwing the baseball.

They'll tell you that it was the mindset.

It was the visualization, the preparation that really led them to this victory on the ball field.

Yet most entrepreneurs and practice owners go about their lives really spinning their wheels without some kind of a solid framework for growth and for setting growth goals and having a positive psychology to make it happen for them.

You know we get trapped into this thinking that it's the next three step mail in sequence or the next Facebook strategy or search engine optimization or the next employee that we hire is going to take our practice to the next level of massive growth.

But really, it's the mindset and a powerful psychology needed so that we can open up all the growth possibilities, getting us out of this tunnel vision and then if we take that tunnel vision and get out into a wider view and we buttress that by a solid blueprint for implementing that growth that's the real determinant for our growth success.

Look, I'm sure you can relate to this, that we as entrepreneurs at one time or another have all had this tunnel vision, that slows the growth of our practice.

Sometimes it's fear based, sometimes it's downright ignorance but it's that slow growth that stops our practice from growing it and puts us in this dead stop.

You know, I remember not long ago… it seemed like it wasn't that long ago.

It's been a few years now but when I was one of my industrial repair company I had at the time only one salesperson, this guy was my entire sales staff.

It was all on his shoulders. And at the time I thought that's all I needed. I was pretty ignorant I wasn't really aware and we were doing OK.

The business was growing a little bit.

Things were really going fine until one day I'm checking my e-mail and I ran across an email that was intended to only go to that one sales guy, but it was accidentally CC'd to me also.

That e-mail was an offer for employment for him.

You know my one and only sales guy, the guy was that I relied on so much was being head hunted by my biggest competitor.

And I was mortified. I was completely surprised at this. This one guy that he was with me for years. We were doing great, but he was considering going work for my competitor. I was completely ignorant completely unaware of the possibilities of losing this key employee.

Now his leaving wasn't his problem. It was my problem this problem was not an employment problem or sales problem it was me having this tunnel vision problem.

I simply wasn't aware my mind had become so closed off that these new ideas on growing my business that I foolishly left myself unaware that him leaving and me being without a salesperson was even a possibility.

It was my fault for thinking that this linear growth model was the one and only way for me to grow at all.

It was really then and only then that I realized that I should have been thinking more about continuing to grow my business in new and different ways instead of becoming comfortable and not limit myself to that only one linear growth model that I was using at a time.

I should have been able to open up and think about growing the business and constantly making myself aware of new ways to grow it and unfortunately for me it took this almost disastrous event to force me to open my mind and get ready and ripe to even consider better growth opportunities.

It took this to get my get my mind right.

I guess so to speak. So, what Sam and I want to do is to help you to not have to go through this kind of pain before you get your mind right before you realize that you are in tunnel vision mode right now because of either fear and you're intentionally keeping yourself in this only one growth mode.

Or because of a lack of awareness and you're probably unintentionally keeping yourself in this tunnel vision mode and you just don't know what you don't know.

Sam Frentzas

I agree with you Walter and I know exactly that deflated feeling because allowed that to happen to me.

Not only that but I felt like I sought out after somebody and tell them exactly my fear and I found the most negative person I could find.

So he can reaffirm my fear and then I can basically lock the door shut the key door and sit in the dark and not allow myself to grow or do anything and say this was it.

So, when I left the stock market traders like me, you know, were walking away from the business.

How many people do you know that were in those trading pits screaming and yelling and making a career that way.

So now I find myself a new career. So, I was recruited to work as many traders were to a financial firm because of my skills and knowledge that basically follow the crowd and did what others were doing.

A few months went by and I showed my personal portfolio to an analyst and that's what it was that really changed everything for me because I was always closed minded.

I can't do that in this business. So again, I follow the crowd did this and I guess this was going to be my career.

I didn't want to sit in front of a computer and just watch stocks all day.

You put in your stock trade and you hold that for months or even years.

He's the one that opened up my eyes.

Now I created the little niche, a better mousetrap shall we say. Let me get this straight. I did not find a way to beat the stock market. If I did we wouldn't be sitting here having this conversation. For the little niche that I was in, what I was able to do is get results faster and help traders with my screening process for small cap stocks.

Great little price. And it worked really well. But what happened was is that this opened up my mind to the possibilities. I got off that train and a month later I quit.

I was able to go ahead and explore all the skills and knowledge that I have and I didn't let fear cripple me any more I didn't let fear say you can't.

Once I saw the possibilities that were out there and saw that others were doing it I realized that I can do it too.

Walter Bergeron

We talk about this awareness that you know you were....there was a big market change that caused you to be aware that you need to make some major changes and open yourself up to growing your own life and your own business.

And that's one definitely one side that keeps you in this tunnel vision mode and then other side really is this fear and fear comes in a lot of different forms and causes you to do a lot of different things.

I mean you know I'm sitting here an my office and I have this picture on the shelf of my library and it's a family photo and it serves as this bittersweet reminder of the tunnel vision that I had at that time and how fear did two things fear.

Fear both gave me the tunnel vision but also drove me to a solution that night and to get my mind right in and help me make a life altering decision that I couldn't continue going working for myself.

Working myself into this early grave because I didn't have a clear path a clear vision of growing my business. This was back in 2007, 13 plus years ago my wife Jana and I we were working yet another long weekend and we're having takeout pizza for dinner. And you now the focal point was our son. This picture is my 4-year-old son and he's smiling from ear to ear. He's having a great time eating pizza while he sits in my workbench in our workshop in my industrial repair company. So, imagine a 4-year-old boy with pizza sauce smeared all over his face.

You know that's pretty common for 4 year olds when they eat anything he smeared all over her face and he has a white T-shirt on of course.

He's got big red handprints made compliments of all the red marinara sauce and he's just this huge mess. But he's smiling from ear having this great time because he gets to have pizza. He gets to have dinner with mom and dad at work and he loves doing this. We did it pretty much every Sunday, at least. And fairly often even between those days the week and each time you got to sit at my workbench and he would giggle and have a great time making this huge mess like 4 year olds typically do.

But for me and for my wife on the other side of that camera it was a completely different story.

You see this was the end of yet another full 20 hour weekend. And that was on top of a 60 hour work week and unfortunately really was common for us to have to be at work during these meal times. And we routinely had to order pizza because there was no time to do anything else.

And as I stood there taking that picture there were just tremendous sense of dread, this fear that took over me because I didn't see an end to this. I didn't see another way out. I was locked into the tunnel vision. I designed my business to work me to death through this vicious cycle and I did not have any plan to get out of that vicious cycle I didn't have any plan to get that tunnel vision.

We were going to be working 20 hours every single weekend 60 hours every single week having to eat pizza every single Sunday night until I was 80 years old because I don't have any other way out of this. The path I was taking at that point was definitely the wrong path.

And it was that very night, that very moment that I decided to change the direction of our business so that it could grow much bigger and provide my wife and myself and my son a lifestyle that was worth living.

But it was fear of not knowing other ways to grow the business that was keeping me there. But it is also fear that was driving me out. So, fear is this double-edged sword in some cases. One it can keep you in this tunnel vision but if it's big enough and strong enough it can get you out.

So getting very clear on what you want and even more important what you don't want from your life.

It takes a big effort. And I would encourage you to write it down or to burn this in your head, this image in your head of what you don't want from your life.

I mean for me it's this this picture and this this picture reminds me these fears that I had that kept me to tunnel vision and I hope that you also have the same kind of a picture or an image or conversation that you've written down in your own life and things that you're not willing to accept that will get you out of this tunnel vision that so many of us get in as entrepreneurs.

Sam Frentzas

Yeah Walter and you mentioned a double-edged sword and you're 100 percent correct that this can also work in reverse effect there.

You can paint in an outcome of what you think something's going to be and you have tunnel vision that way without really thinking things through.

So, you know on the other side of that in keeping with the topic of food and talk about a life changing moment.

You know I started the information company and things were going great it was running on autopilot, but it wasn't bringing in the big money, the way I wanted to take care of my family the way I wanted.

And you know I had an idea and without hesitation it a perfect idea, a concept and from there Sam's Beef and Barbecue was born.

I would open one take out place with five tables inside and I could build my empire. Easy right. Should be no problem. I saw I could succeed, so this should be a no brainer. What I didn't think to add is that what I had to put in the time and what I didn't know about the business.

I mean I have no problems rolling up my sleeves and getting to work, it's in my DNA to do that. But what I had was just tunnel vision of an outcome. What I didn't have was the capacity to put everything down to figure out what it's going to take. What I needed to do and to achieve those goals.

Now I had the passion of the outcome but not to sustain in a different industry that I didn't know much about.

Well surprise. Two years later that I couldn't leave the place because it wouldn't run the same without me. And there I was with a newborn and my wife would have my wife would bring my son to the restaurant so I could spend time with him. And there I was spending.   I think this is roughly over a hundred hours a week in this business. So I didn't look at every angle. I mean I never worked in the restaurant business. I just thought I could do it because I succeeded in something else. My tunnel vision was that I can just I can do it. Here's the outcome I could just put some money into it and there it goes.

So, I knew the numbers what I didn't know was the industry and I rushed into something without being aware.

Success in one industry doesn't mean success in another. So for the first time my life it took the first offer that came in and I got out of something because it wasn't a fit for me. That tunnel vision costed me time and money because I didn't think things through correctly.

So I wasn't aware of everything that came into this business. It was what I can get out of it. So that was a mistake I learned from having tunnel vision.

Basically, the opposite way of just rushing into something and thinking I can do it, here's the outcome without thinking things through without being aware of the outcome.

Walter Bergeron

I am so glad you talked about these stories, Sam, and it's so impactful when you can relate these stories to your own life and I know you know those reading and listening to this, can always relate to there's times in our lives we have low points where fear or some lack of awareness stops their business from growing and moving forward.

And it's here in the stories of the low points in someone's life it's very easy for you to make those connections for yourself.

And you know you and I we have some mastermind members and actually they are also part of the inner circle as well.

Jim and Cathy who own an educational services business. They actually tutor underprivileged and kids that have developmental problems on math and reading and a number of different subjects. And Cathy, she has been doing this for many years.

I think gone on our fourth decade of doing this and her and her husband have owned this business for a long time. So when you and I work with them and when we have private discussions you know she shares with me and us her stories of fear and fear of failure.

That's definitely one thing but she went through something a little bit different. Her fear was always of ridicule within her own industry. She's a teacher by trade.

Very well educated and with many years of experience teaching in public schools.

Her fear of ridicule from her own colleagues kept her vision of growing her educational services business only in one direction only doing one thing the entire time.

She's been doing this for a long time so this dates from a bit. But there was a time when she kept thinking that she wanted to take her educational services program and put these lessons online on the Internet at that time of course this is a while back so this date her. But you know that was her big idea.

But since no one else was doing it and she had a fear of ridicule from her colleague's other teachers when they are telling her the only way to teach a kid who is underprivileged or that has developmental and behavioral problems the only way to teach them properly to have them in a desk face to face one on one that's the best way to teach them.

She kind of got into the self-sabotage of the only way for me to do this is just like everyone else is doing it so that's only I'm going to grow my business.

And the reason I'm doing this is because no one else is doing it online. I don't want to be ridiculed by my colleagues my peers in my industry. So I'm going to keep doing this even though I think it's a possibility for good idea.

So that fear can certainly keep you in one mode of growth for your business. She used this term and I'm not sure if this really applies here or not but she talks about the fact that her colleagues only had this one way this one method of teaching that kept her dreams watered down.

She calls it you know this watering down effect of her idea was you know to really blow up her business by taking this thing online.

But she kept watering down her own vision to this tunnel vision of how everyone else was doing it because of that fear.

And so she talks about a lot. And so it's not just you and I know that have this tunnel vision based off appears in this tunnel vision based off a lack of awareness.

One good thing about that is that yeah, it's for everyone else everyone else has these fears.

But the other good thing about this is that this is exactly how we're going to show you how to get out of this and we're not quite there yet to show them exactly how they're going to use these other stories to get them out of this and inspire them to other ways of thinking in other ways of overcoming his business growth tunnel vision.

But I want to let you know that this these stories are truly important. While right now it just seems like we're telling your story so that we can relate to this and know that we understand these fears.

They're also the answer to getting out of these fears and so we get that in a second here.

I know Sam you had one other thing you wanted to talk about before we got to that that answer and having these guys helping them overcome this tunnel vision.

Sam Frentzas

Yeah this is for you guys too. And the reason we are telling you these stories that we're even telling you these personal story is that so the mistakes that we've made is that you don't have to.

You don't have to go through. You don't have to live them. You know here's my story a perfect example of how I got the hell beaten out of me because in one aspect I'm sitting here with all these Harvard educated guys in a financial firm that are these analysts that know everything from everybody and were ridiculing me like you think you could do this.

You were just so trade you there screaming and yelling and you just think you don't have the skill set for this and that crippled me.

Putting something out there a fear of these guys and they were ridiculing me just to the fact that even mentioned it. And I wouldn't even walk past these guys. Once I finally got this thing out there right. These guys are still working at that office and I have the freedom to go ahead and move on and do something else.

So, I let fear crippled me, something that I actually had the credibility to do.

And on the reverse side it was getting into another industry without letting fear slow me down or having that tunnel vision of say I could do anything.

The ridicule, by the way, came afterwards with the "I told you so's" on top of that. So, again with that double-edged sword we're going to help you navigate that. So you guys can find the sweet spot in the middle of getting the big success out of this process. That we're going to with these story that we are telling you.

There is a purpose behind it and we're going to get to it right now so you will find that absolutely valuable.

You're going to see why we're telling you these things. So this is all about how to get your mind set right.

Walter Bergeron

Sam, I know we've been talking about all these fears and this lack of awareness and these are really just kind of, just really some negative stories, some negative messages.

Personally, I believe that fears and these negative messages really are 10 times more powerful than positive messages.

So as an antidote, as a way to get out of this growth tunnel vision, the antidote to all this negative garbage that goes on these fears is to stop you from expanding your tunnel vision and to get into your massive growth opportunities is to seek out and find great examples of entrepreneurs and small business owners that have already overcome these fears, that have already overcome this lack of awareness.

And the antidote is to look for stories of those that have gone on to some great success and really saturate your mind with all these positive messages, so you can overcome these fears. You can overcome this lack of awareness. You can see what others are doing. Me, myself I've always gravitated towards these inspirational stories of overcoming adversity.

I guess I do it for a couple of reasons. For one reason, I find it entertaining. I like listening to these stories.

I really enjoy hearing about these things. There's a series, I'm not sure where it's on. It's a TV series of a show called The Men Who Built America.

And it's five or six stories of guys like Carnegie and Rockefeller and JP Morgan, and they're telling their stories of how they overcome all this adversity and how they overcame all this lack of knowledge in a time when our nation was growing in this great industrial age and how they overcame those things.

To me, that's really entertaining. I mean, not everyone enjoys that or finds it entertaining. So finding these stories of information. For one thing, it's fun, because I like doing it. And really the second thing, and the reason I know I really want to focus on here today is that the reason I want you to saturate your mind with these positive stories, is because this is a way for you to help move past these fears.

Because, look, if these guys, and if you hear their stories of where they came from, they're like immigrants.

They literally got off the boat with just a few cents in their pocket, and then built these tremendous companies at this time in our nation. And I'm even gonna' tell you some stories of guys who are still doing it today.

So it wasn't just limited to way back in the late 1800's and 1900's. These guys built, they're still doing this now. But these massively inspirational stories are a way to help you move past your own fears.

You know, if these guys could overcome their fears, which seem way worse than any fears that I've had myself, then I think to myself, "Well, shoot, if they can do it, so can I." And even when you study more recent entrepreneurs like companies on the, I'm gonna' show you here, the Inc. 500 List, when I studied these massively inspirational stories, I used their ideas for massive growth.

And it helps to make me aware of great new ideas and new ways to grow your business. So, look at these stories and look at saturating yourself with these kinds of messages in two ways. If it doesn't entertain you like it does me, that's fine, too.

But I'm hoping it helps you to see that there are others that have overcome these fears, that have moved past this lack of awareness of other ways to massively grow their business.

Now, look, I know at first it's not easy, especially if you've never done this before.

It's natural, and I know I do it myself. It's natural for you to be threatened. It's natural for you to even be jealous of other successful entrepreneurial stories and to justify why these guys could do it and you can't.

That really is part of the garbage that's in your head that's starting to take over. And like I said before, I think that garbage tends to be ten times more powerful than the positive messages. So as a way to get past that, I want you just to keep reading.

Keep absorbing these messages, these stories, and internalize these messages, not the feelings of jealousy or the feelings of threatening.

Don't internalize that part but internalize the good message of overcoming those fears and finding new and great ways to grow your business.

And it won't always be easy, but keep at it, and that's one way to make sure that you keep moving past this.

And so that's really what the worksheets that Sam and I have here are all about.

These worksheets are about taking your business to the next level by actually studying, and not just passively sitting by and listening to these stories, but truly studying what others are doing and let them inspire you to your own success.

So study their stories. And so the worksheets are designed to help you do that.

You're actually gonna do a serious study of the methods that these entrepreneurs used to get past their fears and to go on to their moments of awareness that helped them grow on to their own massive business growth.

So, I want to do a quick walkthrough of the worksheets. If you've got them here, go ahead and take a look at the worksheets.

All they really are, straightforward and simple, I want you to name the company you're taking a look at.

In this example here, I took a look at Inc. 500 number three. The company is called Gametime. And so,

I want you to sort of, when you go through your examples, write those names down.

Now, Gametime's revenue at the start of this was $148,000 per year. $148,000 per year. For many successful entrepreneurs, they spend that on the cost of their house in a year. But this guy, that's everything he was making a year.

And he built that business, his name was Brad Griffith, he built that business to $48,000,000 and achieved 34,021% growth, and he overcame this huge, huge deficit and grew his business to this level.

So, you want to talk about overcoming some fears, Brad was actually in tunnel vision mode, just like we talked about at the beginning of this training here.

He was in an industry that already had a huge fast pace. He was selling tickets online to events, like baseball and football venues.

He was selling tickets at the last minute, pretty much scalping, I guess, is kind of what they call it, but he was doing it legally, and that was his business.

But he had competitors like Ticketmaster and SeatGeek and Stubhub.

These are multi-billion dollar companies that he's competing against. Imagine the fear that Brad had thinking about, "How in the hell am I gonna overcome what these guys are doing?" And so that's what the worksheet's about.

I want you to find inspirational stories like that.

Write down the fears that those entrepreneurs overcome, and then think about internally about what fears you're trying to overcome to grow your business, to open up your mind, to get out of that tunnel vision.

For Brad, he had this fear of going against huge competitors like these guys. I mean, can you imagine if somebody came into your area that could just stomp you into the dirt on a whim, they're so big. That's the kind of competition he was against.

But by keeping his mind open, he developed what he calls his ace in the hole. His growth model awareness of software and a customer experience like no others.

So what he did, and this is what opened up his business to be able to grow it over 34,000%, this was his moment of awareness like we have on the worksheet.

His moment of awareness is when he actually started sitting at the seats that he was selling.

He would go to the ballpark, and he would sit at those sits and take pictures of what the view was of those actual seats.

So the tickets he would sell, he would actually put his customers in the mindset of what would happen when they bought the ticket, what they would see when they bought the ticket.

And he'd used professional photographers, and eventually he hired his own staff to go and take these pictures, but he opened his mind up to the other growth models and began this meteoric rise in revenue from $148,000 to $48,000,000, because he was able to open up his mind, get past his fear of being a competitor of these huge multi-billion dollar companies that could stomp him at a whim and grow his business well beyond that.

And so his moment of awareness was when he realized that he could overcome this just with a great idea.

But he could have never had done that had he let his fears overcome him and be down and negative, because he was in an industry that was growing but was being overtaken by these huge companies.

So find these inspirational stories, and then imagine what your business would look like if you overcame your own fears, if you embraced your moments of awareness, and if you had this kind of growth.

That's the power of these inspirational stories and how they're gonna help you get past all these things on your own and open up your tunnel vision to a wide view of how you can massively grow your very own business.

Sam Frentzas

Yeah. And Walter, that is a great point. We want to concentrate on that word fear.

And these stories are not just for inspiration, they're for you to get nuggets of information out of and see what others have done and what path they took.

Now, I can pretty much guarantee that this next guy we're going to have a fun story with, and the reason why I'm going to talk about him, and what I love about this story is that he wouldn't let fear stop him.

Okay? Out of every successful business owner, they had to overcome fear to get where they are.

For him, failure was not an option. So I love the story of John Paul DeJoria. So here's a guy who invented a better shampoo way back in the day.

The biggest thing was, you only had to use it once to get the same result as other shampoos that had to use it twice on your head.

So to him, this was right. He didn't care, and if you haven't figure out who this guy is or what is product is, it's Paul Mitchell Shampoo. I bet you, even at one point in your life, used it. And here's a guy who's living out of his car going from salon to salon to sell his product.

And I don't think I mentioned this, but his young son was living with him out of his car.

So, I mean, nobody would have thought that this guy to go get a job and try to earn what he can and support his son and make a great living, because at this point he was just living out of his car and his shampoos were in the trunk.

All his money was going towards his product. But he didn't let fear stop him.

He knew what he had was better, and he built, and he built, and he didn't let fear cripple him and stop him in any which way.

Which, a lot of us, we get to a certain point and fear kicks in, and we're done.

We figure we throw up the red flag and say ... Or the white flag, excuse me, and say that's it for us. I've had enough. I quit. So that did not stop him.

So I'm sure none of you right now are sitting in your car listening to this or living out of your car listening to this coming up with an idea or having your own product and letting fear stop you, because other things are coming up.

Now, what I love about this, he is sitting right now in his $50,000,000 estate in Malibu with all the toys a man could want, because he didn't let fear stop him.

So what I love also about this thing is that not only is it a rags to riches story, but he's saying the pledge giving 50% of his earnings to better the world.

If you can see what he has done and the road he took, fear didn't stop him.

So fear should not stop you from knocking on those doors, pushing even harder, because this is exactly what you need to see and get that nugget of information. Even if it's just one that'll propel you to that next level.

Walter Bergeron

I'm so glad you told that story, Sam. Not everyone can grow to have companies that size.

And even when I like to watch that show, The Men Who Built America, these guys are growing it to what are essentially the largest companies in the world.

And so it doesn't necessarily take you growing to that level to know that you have to overcome this fear.

I mean, this works for everyday businesses, even businesses that are growing, like this example I'm going to give you here, this business grew to $12,000,000.

Not a tremendous business, not an earth-shattering amount of business, but he made it to number 21 on the Inc. 500 List, and his name was Armir Harris, and he owns a company called Shofur. He actually leases out buses and has a software that allows places to be able to lease out large numbers of vehicles. And so if you read his story, and that's what I want you guys to do.

I want you to go and study these entrepreneurs and see what they're doing to overcome their fears and to have their moments of awareness.

If you go to the Inc. 500 List, the very first 15, 20, I think even more than that will have a good long write up of what these entrepreneurs did and how these companies became so successful and grew so fast. Armir here grew to number 21 in three years. His growth rate was 10,448%. 10,000% growth.

This is a guy who not just a few years earlier was a political refugee in Albania, was forced to come to the United States with $2,000 between his entire family. He started his business with only 800 bucks. So, imagine the fear of being homeless in a brand new country and a language that you don't speak with no money. He was a young lad. I think he was still in his teens. So, he had no real education. His family was a bunch of political refugees also, but they were very entrepreneurial, so he got to try his hand at number of businesses.

He started a real estate business. That failed. A taxi company. That failed. He tried to become a pro tennis player. That failed. So, he had all these failures and these fears that he came to this country with, but he was still able to make it to this list, not because he let this keep banging him down and beating him into the dirt, it was because he overcame these fears, and he had moments of awareness where he could take these opportunities and grow his businesses. And not all of his businesses succeeded.

We're talking about success here, yes, but to get to this level of success probably took him four, five, six businesses to get to this level. So, don't expect this to happen overnight. But you know it's still something you have to overcome.

You still have to overcome these fears no matter what you're gonna do. And so saturate your mind. Study these stories of inspiration from these entrepreneurs so that you can hold yourself accountable to doing this.

Put down a name, the revenue. Put down the growth percentage so you can see just how fast these companies are growing. Imagine putting your growth rate of, maybe it's a few percent per year, maybe it's 30% per year.

Put that next to a number like 10,448% and see how inspired you get to grow your business. Knowing that you're growing at maybe 100%. Maybe you're doubling the size of your business every year, but realize that this guy's doing it thousands of times more than you are.

Not because he's better, not because he's better looking, not because he speaks their language better, he's better educated, none of those things.

It was simply because he overcame these fears and took advantage of the ability to see and to open his mind up to all the different growth opportunities that his business and his industry allowed him.

And then write down the moments of awareness.

For Armir, his moments of awareness came when he saw that the Democratic National Convention didn't have enough buses to transport all their people.

They needed like 60 buses or something. And so he realized that he could figure out a solution for him.

So, his moment of awareness was no way existed for someone to rent 60 freaking buses and go across the country for two weeks.

But him being an entrepreneurial spirit and overcoming his fears and being able to open himself up to this being aware of a way to grow a business, he was able to quickly develop a quick software that just combined access to all these bus companies and, bam, a business was born, a business that's now doing $12,000,000 a year and growing at 10,000% over three years.

So, imagine what your business would look like if you were able to overcome the fears that you have, if you were able to pinpoint the moments of awareness in your own business that could be life-changing for you.

And maybe your story can inspire others for success. So, do yourself a favor right now. Don't do anything else before you start studying these companies of success.

Saturate your mind with all this ability of others to overcome these fears and this lack of awareness, and let it help you to do the same thing for your business and your life.

And know that just because things are going okay right now, that may just be a sign that you're not fully aware of all the opportunity out there.

So, even if you think you're doing well, even if your business is growing, hell, maybe your one of the people on the Inc. 500 List.

You know there are still moments of awareness, and there are things that and methods of growing your business that you may not be aware of. Open your mind up, even if you're doing well, to these stories of success and do the homework. Study what these companies are doing. Do the worksheets.

Write this down, and I can just about promise you that you're gonna be able to have the opportunity to grow your business in bigger ways also.

Sam Frentzas

That is actually a great point, Walter.

And I think another thing, another topic that we need to talk about, another fear that nobody is really thinking of is fear of competition.

And this is another fear right now of trying to keep the whole thing to yourself and not letting anybody in.

One thing I love about The Men Who Built America, I actually love that show, too, is their biggest thing was fear of competition, right? Five of the guys that moved America, their biggest fear was competition, and they squashed it at every place they can.

And what happened at the end, it turned to be from competition to collaboration.

It ended up becoming bigger and bigger collaborating than trying to buy this guy out that's doing the same thing or maneuver, because they were spending more time against their competition than it was in their own business.

And if you start down that path, it becomes less of what you're doing and more about they're doing.

What's great about at the end is that they fought so hard to acquire such massive wealth, at the end they were fighting each other on who could give the most away. So I love that part of it. And here we go back to the early 1900's learning that lesson.

And I think we could take a story of our own Mastermind member, Gene Kelly, who started API with the mission of creating 100,000 careers for plumbers, electricians, especially when you see with the fires going on in California, it's a big need.

It was, "I want to be the first in this space and do something online and go to the masses with it." So he didn't want any competition. But what he realized was collaborating with a couple of other Mastermind members, he could take this to the masses.

With John Tucker and Dr. Kalaras from QTI and John Tucker again from Choice Career College, that mission changed from, "I'm just doing this on my own to collaborating seeing that they can work together and go on this mission to create 100,000 careers for veterans.

And now it's not going to be local. It's not just one thing. This is going to be nationwide.

They realize that ... And they do each in their own space but collaborating together instead of competing against each other trying to say, "Mine is better than yours," realizing that, "What you're doing might not be a fit for this guy, but it might be a fit for him," and vice versa.

Somebody might see him and say, "Well, I don't want to be trained as doing cyber security, but man I love working with my hands in plumbing." So you're able to help somebody, which is great. But you're bringing more eyes on the team that you're working with.

So guys that might not be a fit for you are a fit for them, and guys that aren't a fit for them might be a fit for you. By collaborating, they're able to escalate their businesses to levels that they couldn't do it on their own, because they would be sitting there spending more time competing with each other and maybe not the correct message comes across.

By collaborating, this changes everything. So, the biggest thing we want to stress now, don't have that fear of competition if there is a possibility for collaboration. This just opens up more doors, more joint ventures, more opportunities.

Same thing happened, as I told the story earlier, with the Paul Mitchell shampoos. As he started to grow, more opportunities were there. Then he goes into the tequila, so I'm sure all of us have had Jose Cuervo tequila. So, these opportunities as he's getting bigger, more resources are seeking him out, because of his vet collaboration.

So, one thing you want to get out of the mindset of is that you can't let anybody near this or you're competition. If there's an opportunity for collaboration, keep an open mind and see if there's something out there for you to collaborate, and now you're increasing your business. At the end of the day, it's massive revenue growth.

So getting in the mindset of, "Well, I gotta watch who my competition is, and this is only for me," is there a possibility for a collaboration, and this becomes now where he wanted to do one thing, John Tucker wanted to do another thing and Dr. Kalaras wanted to do another thing, they don't have the spirit of competition anymore. Now they've collaborated and are on one mission together.

So that cohesiveness will net them a lot more working together than with them trying to compete against each other. And who wins out of this? The veterans. Walter, I know that you're a veteran yourself. I know this means a lot to you. Get to working on everything.

Chapter 7

You've Got Questions

Frequently Asked Questions

Does it matter how large my database is?

Salesfuze App is a full feature HIPAA compliant, powerful customer resource management (CRM) platform giving you the ability to automate all of your current and future marketing and sales processes and track your results in real time with full transparency. It includes text, email, voicemail, video, website, images, phone calls, call recording, scheduling software, calendars, webforms, KPI dashboard, complete 3rd party integrations, patient surveys, webinars, seminars, appointments, …and the list goes on, this is complete and comprehensive and no one else has it all like Salesfuze! If you have a large or small list of leads, this will work. With a very large list of thousands of leads, we want you to choose the newest leads that you have been in contact with during the last 12 months to start with. If your list is only a few hundred contacts, that's fine too. As long as you have the availability for appointments, agree with our offer, and sustain the patients that we book for your practice, you will see results! Every 30 days, we will create a new offer to stay engaged with them.

I want new leads, what about getting me some new leads?

Ok, we'll get you there after the first month, but to start out, it is best to for us to focus on the goldmine you have sitting dormant in your inactive patient list to bring your practice immediate sale success. In 30 days, we'll introduce you to some spectacular services to get you those new leads you want, we promise.

How many appointments can I expect to get from Salesfuze?

The number of appointments we set per month will depend on the quality of your list and the relationship you have with them. If you have had recent contact with your list and you have good relationship with them, you can expect as many as 50 appointments per month. If you have not had contact with your list recently or do not have a good relationship with them you can expect as little as 10 appointments per month. We will adjust the number of leads we send texts to get you at least 10 appointments per month as time goes on.

Will you send out reminders to appointments that we book?

With Salesfuze, we have our own booking platform that takes care of the appointments we book. We send reminders to the appointments that we book, not the patients booked by your staff.

Why can't I put my appointments into Salesfuze too?

Salesfuze is a *Live* conversation between a new patient and our Live sales agent and not simply an automated out of the box form of automation, therefore, we would have no history of a conversation with the appointments your staff has booked, which would make it less-personable when nurturing those leads.

What happens if you double book me?

What a great problem to have, right? We can handle this one of two ways, depending on your preference. We can immediately rebook them for an alternate time. Many of our clients prefer to keep the double booking and just make the time for them when they arrive. Just let us know which method you prefer!

I absolutely cannot be double booked!

No problem! Simply provide us with a timeframe that we are able to book appointments for you. If we get a patient that we are unable to book during your limited times, we will call you personally and get another time if possible. If this happens frequently we will get with you and come up with a more appropriate schedule that suits both your needs as well as your patients needs.

What happens if you don't get me any appointments?

It's never happened but just in case we don't get you 12 appointments in the first 30 days, you will receive another month of Salesfuze at no charge and we will get you those 12 appts that we promised.

How much manpower will I need to use Salesfuze?

No extra manpower needed; we actually take some load off your staff by doing the appointment booking for them. All they need to do is to update our calendar with the outcome of the appointments, which takes about 5 seconds per appointment, really... 5 seconds.

This seems like a lot of work on my intake person/staff?

This actually takes less time than it would take your staff to set up an appointment normally, because we handle the conversation. All your staff needs to do is open an email and put the appointment into your software. Otherwise they would spend lots of time on the phone talking about the offer, trying to convince the lead to schedule. We have a professional sales staff that keeps your professional reputation at the forefront while focusing on getting an appointment booked. Your staff only does this part time, we do it 24/7/365 and know how to do this the right way.

Will this replace my own appointment setting software?

No, this is not meant to replace anything that you currently use to track you own appointment setting efforts. You will need to continue using your current appointment setting process in addition to updating these leads with their appointment outcomes.

When is the best time to send out my offer?

We have found through vast testing that Tue, Wed & Thur from 10:30am-Noon are by far the most successful times to send out texts, due to the larger response rates. We highly recommend you stick to these days and times if you expect great results!

What's Next? What happens after you send this offer to my entire list?

Then we create a new irresistible offer to your client list. It is important to do this at least every 90 day, but we never want to put a halt to the follow-ups. *Forever Follow-Up* is critical to making sure you mine every bit of value from your list.

What happens if they call about the texted offer?

When your client happens to call the number Salesfuze uses to text your database (because it happens), the call will be forwarded to your main office. In this instance, simply book the call and let us know, so that we can send them reminder texts for their upcoming appointment! It is very important, that your staff knows about the offer to better increase the amount of bookings.

Can I send out more than 1 offer at a time?

Each Salesfuze account is set up to handle 1 offer per list, which is 2500 leads per month. You can change your offer as soon as the previous offer is completed, then continue to run your list through multiple offers. Or, you can easily purchase another Salesfuze application and we can run 1 additional offer per account.

Why doesn't Salesfuze send out emails?

Have you ever sent out 100 emails and booked 3 appointments from them? Us either. However, we do routinely with live text conversations. Sales (yes, an appointment is a small sale) happen in conversation because people do business with people... you can't have live conversation with email... but you can with text. Not to mention, text has a lower barrier than a phone call or a live meeting.

What we have seen is that email response is less than .1% and voicemail is .03%, but when we combine an irresistible text offer with a live person who can respond within 5 minutes, we can get an appointment about 3% of the time. Now 3% may sound like a tiny number but by having a live person focus on scheduling an appointment via text only, you can increase the possibility of getting an appointment/registration by 30X. *Imagine* getting 30X more appointments/registrations from your marketing efforts with this change!

Why isn't it better to slowly nurture them with education?

What we have seen is that educational materials force your patients to self-diagnose and usually incorrectly. What is much, much more impactful than hoping your patients educate themselves is to have a consultation and spend time with you. You are the expert, not some PDF or video, it's better patient care when they can spend time with you and get a professional opinion. Google is not a doctor, you are!

What happens if appointments don't show up or cancel?

We know how frustrating this can be so if they cancel or they don't show for their appointment, we will send them a string of texts spread out for a few days and we will work hard to get them to re-schedule their appointment.

Practice Growth Review

Monthly we prove or value to your practice by going over the numbers that are most important to your practice and tie them to the most important measuring stick to you – CASH! If what we are doing isn't measurable in money, then we aren't doing our job well enough and we'll make immediate changes to make sure that everything we do is profitable for you. We want to earn your business each and **every month.**

Why Patient Reactivation

- Loyal customers, even if you haven't seen them in a long time are 5x as likely to repurchase, 5x as likely to forgive you for anything you did that they didn't like, 4x as likely to refer and 7x as likely to try a new offering.

- The probability of selling to an existing customer is 60 to 70%, while the probability of selling to a new prospect is only between 5 and 20%.

- Returning Customers Spend 67% More Money Than New Customers and are the only type of patient that can give you referrals.

- On average every referring customers makes an average of 2.68 invites

- Referral Marketing generates 3-5x higher conversion rates than any other channel.

- It's 5x to 25x more expensive to get a new client

Why Texting Works

- Open rates for texts vary between 90 to 98%, emails are clinging to 8 to 10% meaning that texts are more than 900% more likely to be viewed.

- There's a 10x decrease in your odds of making a contact with a lead after the first 5 minutes; waiting 15 minutes meant losing nearly 91% of your potential leads.

- Responding in 5 minutes vs 10 minutes shows a 400% increase in your odds of qualifying a new lead

- The #1 preferred channel for customer service in the US is messaging vs telephone calls

- With 92% satisfaction, live chat is preferred to more traditional channels, like phone or email

- Live chat leads to a 48% increase in revenue and a 40% increase in conversion rate as opposed to automated chats and emails.

- Researchers say that 32% of recipients respond to SMS offers. Around 50% of US consumers who receive branded SMS texts go on to make direct purchases.

Why follow up?

- If you text a contact 3 or more times after first contact, they are 328% more likely to convert to a sale

- You are 100x more likely to connect with an inbound lad if you follow up in the first 5 minutes.

- You are 200% more likely to connect with any lead if you space your follow up time no more than 1 day apart.

Chapter 7/You've Got Questions

- Nurtured Leads make 47% larger purchases than non-nurtured leads

- 44% of sales people give up after 1 follow up attempt

- 92% of sales people quit after they are told NO only 4 times; however 80% of prospects say NO 4 times before they say YES